Praise for
Sapphires and Other Precious Jewels

"In *Sapphires and Other Precious Jewels,* Terri McFaddin shows that she is one of the most gifted communicators of our time. She combines her own life experiences and understanding of women with her profound knowledge of the Bible to inspire each of us to reach our divinely designed potential. Through the use of wonderful stories, in-depth studies of fascinating women of the Bible, and comparisons of feminine qualities to precious stones, this book speaks to the reader on many different levels."

—MARILYN MCCOO, entertainer

"*Sapphires and Other Precious Jewels* is an inspirational goldmine for the many women of color who struggle to know and accept their true worth in the eyes of God. Terri McFaddin sensitively challenges African-American women to embrace biblical truths that will both elevate and empower them. Imaginative and profoundly compassionate, *Sapphires* is a treasure."

—RONN ELMORE, PSY.D., author of *How to Love a Black Man*

"Terri McFaddin is one of the best-kept secrets in the world of ministry today. Her profound understanding of the word of God and her ability to creatively bring its principles to life as she speaks profound truths into the hearts of women is life-changing. Uncovering old mind-sets of corrupted self-esteem to reveal the jewels we are within, *Sapphires and Other Precious Jewels* will cause those who read it to finally be loosed to celebrate the handiwork of God in their lives and embolden them to embrace their purpose with new determination."

—MICHELLE MCKINNEY HA
of the Proverbs 31 Man

"Terri McFaddin takes a new and fresh approach to celebrating the uniqueness of Black women. This book is a jewel that should be read several times, then recommended to others with great enthusiasm!"

—ALAINA REED HALL, film and television actress

"*Exquisite* is the first word that comes. *Sapphires and Other Precious Jewels* magnificently reminds us of truths that have been relegated (by history and society) to the dark, back rows of our spirits—truths that reveal our divinely ordained place in the universe."

—MARIA DOWD, founder and executive producer
of *African American Women on Tour*

Sapphires

AND OTHER

Precious Jewels

Sapphires

AND OTHER

Precious Jewels

DISCOVER AND CELEBRATE THE BEAUTY OF

WOMEN OF AFRICAN DESCENT

TERRI McFADDIN

WATERBROOK
PRESS

SAPPHIRES AND OTHER PRECIOUS JEWELS
PUBLISHED BY WATERBROOK PRESS
2375 Telstar Drive, Suite 160
Colorado Springs, Colorado 80920
A division of Random House, Inc.

ISBN 1-57856-599-5

Library of Congress Cataloging-in-Publication Data
McFaddin, Terri.
    Sapphires and other precious jewels : discover and celebrate the beauty of women of African descent / Terri McFaddin.— 1st ed.
        p. cm.
Includes bibliographical references.
        ISBN 1-57856-599-5
    1. African American women—Religious life. 2. Self-esteem in women. 3. African American women—Life skills guides. 4. Precious stones—Miscellanea. I. Title.
        BR563.N4M34 2004
        248.8'43'08996073—dc22   2003022361

Printed in the United States of America
2004

10 9 8 7 6 5 4 3

To my prayer partners,
Janet Bailey and Marilyn Beaubien,
two precious jewels.

What would I have done without you?

And to Frank Wilson,
a faithful man of God,
my mentor, brother, friend, and co-laborer in Christ.

You are rare jewel indeed.

Contents

Acknowledgments

A special thanks to Michelle McKinney Hammond—Super Sister and Friend, Adrienne Ingrum—Super Editor, and Pat Ashley and Bunny Wilson—my co-laborers in Christ.

To my most precious jewels, my daughters, Roslyn McFaddin Ballard and Theresa Adam McFaddin.

Thank you, Bishop Kenneth C. Ulmer, pastor and teacher, for sharing your knowledge of the Word and for challenging me to keep learning and growing.

Thank you, Dr. John Goldingay, professor of Old Testament, Fuller Theological Seminary. You are the coolest and most brilliant teacher ever. It's a blessing to sit at your feet.

To Women's Discipleship Group, thank you for showing up! Janet Bailey, Marilyn Beaubien, Renee Brooks, Janice Boyce, Carolyn Brown, DeBorrah Carter, Connie Cole, Andrea B. Cook, Marilyn McCoo Davis, Tammy Dickerson, Starletta DuPois, Denise Edwards, Karen Evans, Sheila Frazier, Helen Harris, Alaina Reed Hall, Deidra Hampton, Denise Hampton, Deneen Hadley, Diane Henry, Elaine Jackson, Judi Jenkins, Angela Jones, Leigh Dupree-Jones, Tane Kester, Miki King, Jalila Larsuel, Joan Carter-Lee, Dena LeMmons, Tegra Little, Sandra Lord, Araceli Montano, Roxanne Nelson, Nicole M. Palmer, Deborah Peques, Cassandra Pipion, Rose Robinson, Desiree Rollins, Gwen Rollins, Marilyn Rouzan, Juanita Scott, Rosie Sicre, Deya Smith, Cheryl Sweeney, Fatimah Thomas, Carolyn Tomlin, Pam Trotter, Camille Tucker, Shelley Wallace, Lethe Ward, Stasia Washington, Constance Williams.

To Sisters Inspiring Sisters, my daughters in the Lord. The Word works!

Here Comes Ms. Sapphire

Here comes Ms. Sapphire—cut from the Rock of Ages
Shaped by adversity into a gem of great price
Hand polished by love into a jewel of thanksgiving

Her heart so big and beautiful
That admirers pass through a rainbow of emotions:
Love
Respect
Admiration
I wanna be a Sapphire too! Just like you!

Fearless and bold, set in pure gold
Laughing at her flaws, standing in awe
Of God's
Plan
Purpose and
Grace to run her race

Here comes Ms. Sapphire
Pressure and pain—transformed into gain

Shining like a lost coin, found by the Master
Shining like a birthday candle, celebrating a new beginning
Shining like a bolt of lightning, filled with His power
Shining like a camera's flashbulb, picturing the moment when…

Ms. Sapphire lifts her head, squares her shoulders
Points her nose and plants her toes in the direction of victory

Here comes Ms. Sapphire
Rare…Valuable…Beautiful…Desirable

Where is her place and what is she worth?
God calls her Co-Ruler of the universe

Introduction

The New Sapphire

Discovering Your New Identity

You may or may not recognize the double meaning of the word *sapphire* in the title of this book. You may think of a sapphire as a beautiful, dark blue gemstone. A jeweler would tell you that sapphires come in a variety of colors and are second only to diamonds in brilliance and hardness. Sapphires are also valued for their rich color and rarity.

And without a doubt sapphire is a fitting metaphor to describe the beauty and value of women of African ancestry. Like sapphires, we come in a variety of colors, and we have a reputation for enduring incredible hardship. Through trials and testing, we continue to shine and maintain our brilliance.

But *sapphire* also bears a negative connotation. The stereotypical image of a loud, ill-tempered Black woman who has a love-hate relationship with men looms in stark contrast to the beauty and brilliance of the gemstone. The stigma dates back to the long-running *Amos 'n' Andy* radio and television program. First aired on radio in 1928, it became a hit television show in 1951. The comedy was about a group of Black people and the challenges they faced after migrating from the Deep South to New York City in search of a better life.

Civil Rights groups strongly opposed this degrading depiction of Black people and Black family life, but despite protest, the series had soaring television ratings, second only to the *I Love Lucy* show. Sapphire Stevens, played by Ernestine Wade, was the lead female character. With her smooth coffee complexion, attractive face, and thick black hair molded into finger waves with greasy pomade, Sapphire was physically appealing, but she was not acknowledged as such by the script. Instead Sapphire was portrayed as a real piece of work.

Married to a lovable con artist called George "Kingfish" Stevens, played by Tim Moore, Sapphire set out to reform her wayward husband with every scheme she could conjure up. To make matters worse, Sapphire had the full-time, unsolicited help of her domineering mother. "Mama" was depicted as a grumpy, overbearing woman who had a special gift for emasculating Black men.

The Sapphire image reached radio listeners and television viewers around the world for nearly thirty years. Episodes of the *Amos 'n' Andy* show were aired in Europe, Ghana, Nigeria, and many Caribbean countries until Civil Rights activists and declining ratings forced the show off the airways in 1953. Even so, the show remained in syndication well into the 1960s, and it created a menacing stereotype that remains engraved in the minds of many today.

Even after the demise of *Amos 'n' Andy*, the public image of Black women continued to be damaged by media portrayals. In *The Color Purple*, Whoopi Goldberg received an Oscar nomination for her portrayal of Celie, a downtrodden Black woman who was despised and abused by her husband. In the same movie Oprah Winfrey played Sofia, a domineering woman who settled her marital disputes by fistfights with her husband,

Harpo. Black women have been maliciously portrayed as sexually immoral, often as prostitutes and drug addicts. At best we have been perceived as a community of welfare recipients and domestics.

I am thankful for women like Phylicia Ayers-Allen who brought redemption to the image of Black women as the leading lady of *The Cosby Show*. Her character, Clair Huxtable, was a successful attorney, supportive wife, and compassionate mother.

Beyond the public arena, countless unsung heroes of African descent quietly play their real-life roles with unwavering faith in God, breakthrough prayer, and unconditional love. I am persuaded that we would have never survived as a people without such women.

It is for these women and countless others who look up to them that I've written this book. *Sapphires and Other Precious Jewels* is intended to help women of color discover and celebrate "The New Sapphire." She is the woman who has been formed out of the heat and pressure of adversity and has emerged as God's polished jewel—the Sapphire of great price.

It is time to tell Sapphire's true story, to share her secrets of victory and pass her baton to the next generation of Black women. We will discover and celebrate the rich deposits of power and creativity that God has poured into the heart of every devalued woman who embraces Jesus as Lord and Savior. As you read, rest in the knowledge that you have been given a wonderful promise of grace and glory that will one day be fully realized.

The LORD their God will save them on that day
as the flock of his people.
They will sparkle in his land
like jewels in a crown.
How attractive and beautiful they will be!
ZECHARIAH 9:16-17, NIV

Chapter 1

Time, Heat, and Pressure

The Making of a Gemstone

I liken you, my darling, to a mare
harnessed to one of the chariots of Pharaoh.
Your cheeks are beautiful with earrings,
your neck with strings of jewels.

SONG OF SONGS 1:9-10, NIV

Ruby-red lips, pearly-white teeth, and eyes that sparkle like diamonds are just a few of the metaphors that have been used to describe beautiful women. But how often do we stop to think about what it is that causes women of African ancestry to shine with the brilliance of rare jewels? Does it all boil down to having the right hair and lips, skin and hips? Or is it something that radiates from a woman's soul that is more powerful than physical appearance?

Looking through the window of a jewelry store at a variety of valuable rings, necklaces, and bracelets, we know that it's more than what we see on the surface that makes these jewels so costly. An expert must study each jewel in order to determine its true worth. A trained eye knows that there is a story of a long and difficult journey hidden in the heart of each beautiful stone. It is the personal story that will determine the value of the jewel. There are no shortcuts, fake enhancements, or makeovers that can duplicate the richness of the emerald, the fire of the black opal, or a Black woman who is truly beautiful.

It is the journey from the depths of the earth that forge the rare and unique qualities that make you—a woman of African ancestry—so valuable. People might have treated you like worthless rock and dirt. Many people missed opportunities for spiritual wealth because they did not recognize your true worth. But as the Lord takes you through the process that will give you a radiance that will never fade, one day people who didn't recognize your value are going to say, "That can't be the same Black girl who used to work in the school cafeteria and took classes at night!" Once your beautiful gifts begin to shine, the world will stop and take notice.

The creation of a beautiful Black woman is not very different from that of a precious jewel. It involves three stages: First the basic gemstone develops as a result of *time, heat, and pressure.* The second stage is refining; the rough gemstone becomes a smooth jewel by skillful *cutting and polishing.* The third stage is placing the jewel in the perfect *design and setting,* and it requires great creativity.

TIME, HEAT, AND PRESSURE

When carbon, iron, and other ordinary minerals in the earth are exposed to high temperatures and extreme pressure over a long period of time, they crystallize into what we know as gemstones. Diamonds, the hardest of all gemstones, are often brought to the earth's surface by violent volcanic eruptions.

Likewise, what is rare and valuable in Black women is developed by time, heat, and pressure and even volcanic upheavals in their personal lives. Countless women who endured tremendous pressures were transformed into shining jewels. These women remind me of the story of the amazing Arabian horses.

Long ago, deep in the Arabian Desert, dwelled sheepherders and horse breeders known as the Bedouins. These nomadic tribesmen were fiercely independent and often warred with rival clans. They fought in the desert heat, and the strength or weakness of a warrior's horse made the difference between victory and defeat.

To maintain their dominance, the Bedouins needed a warrior horse that was strong, courageous, and invincible. The trainers carefully selected the very best of the new foals. In the first year the trainers pampered the horses like their own children. The young animals were watered, fed, and kept in shaded stalls, away from the rays of burning sunlight. The Bedouins purchased Egyptian barley that grew around the fertile crescent of the Nile River. This grain was extremely rich in nutrients and ensured the proper growth of what would become a new breed of horse.

In the second year the young horses began their battle training, which was presented to them as a joyful game rather than a grueling task. Then, at the end of the second year, the young horses faced an abrupt and shocking change.

In the Arabian Desert the season known as the "high heat" is a forty-day period when temperatures rise to 140 degrees and even higher and violent east winds create sandstorms. The heat and winds scorch grain and vines and often kill man and beast. The young horses were carefully shaded and wiped down with cool water during the high heat, but after their second year of life, the canopy was removed, exposing the horses to scorching rays of the sun. They were given little food and water. The fierce warriors who once pampered and protected these gentle animals from the harshness of life now drove them into the desert.

Making loud, warlike sounds, the trainers forced the horses to cross the burning sands. During the cruel crossing, some horses went into shock and died. Others collapsed from heat exhaustion and dehydration. Others became weak from the lack of food. The tormented horses broke out in blisters, foamed at the mouth, and were even scorched and blinded by the burning sandstorms. Only a few horses managed to survive the crossing.

On the opposite side of the desert, their wounds healed and their minds settled. The survivors were mated with each other. The beautiful offspring of these valiant horses spilled from the wombs of their mothers and struggled to their feet ready to triumph over life in the Arabian Desert.

Again, the Bedouins cared for these young foals. They fed, nurtured, and trained them for battle. Then, at the end of the second year of life, the trainers stripped them of comforts and forced them to cross the burning sands. Many died, but the horses that survived were mated on the other side of the Arabian Desert.

After years of this unique method of purging, known as "barley and abuse," a new and fierce breed of horse evolved. These Arabian stallions and mares earned a reputation for beauty, strength, and courage. Arabian horses thrived under adversity. They could endure staggering heat and fight battles for days and weeks with very little food or water.

Just as some of the world's most valuable horses were developed in the heat of the Arabian Desert, flawless jewels were mined from Africa. But the real diamonds, sapphires, and rubies were the stolen African people, with dark muscular bodies, woolly hair, flaring nostrils, and ivory teeth. Our ancestors were captured, shackled, and thrust into the furnace of adversity—located in the belly of the slave ships that crossed the Atlantic Ocean—where they would endure the agony of the Middle Passage or die.

Each day of the journey, the captives were taken from the hold of the ships and brought to the top deck to be examined by their captors. Some were half dead from hunger and exhaustion. Some were diseased or had collapsed mentally and emotionally. The weak and dying were tossed overboard while the strong were returned to the bottom of the ship. Over and over again the process was repeated until the Africans who survived the crossing, like the Arabian horses, rested their feet on new lands.

Women of African ancestry were sent to nations around the world where they survived physical and emotional abuse. In spite of overwhelming adversity, they continued to give birth to new generations. The offspring of these women had to become even stronger and tougher.

We who live in this present age are survivors, whether we are at the bottom or the top of the social and economic ladder. As women descended from those who withstood the high heat, we know how to survive. We continue to rise no matter how many times we are pushed down or stumble and fall.

We have endured time, heat, and pressure. We have passed the test of difficult times. We have been purged in the heat of oppression. God has allowed the pressures of our painful history to bring to the surface the best of who we are. Your very existence in this world is a testimony that you belong to a powerful tribe of overcomers.

While the Lord has used time, heat, and pressure to form us into powerful and enduring gemstones, we must bravely move on to the next stage of our "jewel" development. To become spectacular and more valuable, we must be cut and polished.

I consider that our present sufferings are
not worth comparing with the glory
that will be revealed in us.

Romans 8:18, NIV

Chapter 2

The Master of the Gemstone

Cutting and Polishing—the Process of Transformation

> *"They shall be Mine," says the LORD of hosts,*
> *"On the day that I make them My jewels."*
>
> MALACHI 3:17

*I*n order to become a jewel, a gemstone must first be separated from the dull rock and sand that mask its beauty and radiance. Open the door of your imagination and journey with me into the secret world of the lapidary, a person who is skilled in the ancient art of cutting and polishing colorful gemstones.

REVEALING THE BEAUTY WITHIN THE STONE

Let's walk down a long hallway to the small room where Yaqar, a bearded gem cutter, stands at his worktable. Descended from three generations of master lapidaries, Yaqar fastens the belt of his black tunic, adjusts his wire-rimmed glasses, and then devotes his full attention to a dull piece of rock in the center of the table. Next to the jagged rock rests a set of well-worn tools that once belonged to his father and his grandfather before him.

Yaqar touches the rock gently, as a father would approach a frightened child. "Don't be afraid. You are in good hands," he whispers to the gemstone as if it were living. In truth it is alive, but not in the way that people define life. But Yaqar knows that once a gemstone has been transformed into a polished jewel, there is a dialogue between the human heart and the sparkling gem that defies all logic and understanding.

What is it about a piece of shiny stone that makes it so powerfully alive and so desirable that one would offer great wealth to possess it? Yaqar knows this secret and often repeats the revelation to his sons:

"God reached deep into the bosom of the earth and plucked out a precious jewel so that we would remember three important things:

"*God's grace.* A jewel is God's way of giving us what we don't deserve and could never create ourselves.

"*God's glory.* A jewel causes us to shine. It honors and adorns us with beauty and reflects the splendor of God.

"*God's love.* A jewel is a piece of God's heart that is given to us so the world will know we are his beloved."

The uncut gemstone is lying before Yaqar like a crouched woman with dark skin. How does he convince this precious gemstone that, even though there will be pain as he polishes and shapes her into a valued jewel, in the end she will be glad for the journey. He has come not to wound her but to set her free from the jealous rock and dirt that are hiding her beauty.

Yaqar scratches his beard, picks up the stone, and rolls it in the palm of his hand. He studies its weight and texture. He wonders if there will be deep cracks, secret pockets, and knots inside the stone that will cause it to shatter under the pressure of transformation. Yaqar takes a deep breath. He carefully scrapes away a first portion of the outer crust. He can almost feel the stone wrenching in pain as the instrument digs into the surface.

Finally, the light and the gem meet for the first time. The bright rays dance across the surface of the stone, and it glistens with fire.

The master lapidary picks up another cutting tool and whispers a prayer that the swift blow he is about to deliver to the center of the gemstone will not cause the stone to shatter into pieces. He raises his hand and delivers the stroke with precision and confidence.

The pieces of the stone lie on his table in broken disarray like a woman who has suddenly lost her reason for existence, separated from a loving relationship, career severed, a family member dead. But now the part of the gem that will shine the brightest is fully exposed. Yaqar picks up the broken stone that will be soon become his masterpiece. He will grind and shape to completely remove cracks and flaws. He will sand and polish until he creates a multifaceted jewel that will reflect light and color with such brilliance that the world will stand in breathless awe. "I will afflict you no more. Now I will break their yoke from your neck and tear your shackles away" (Nahum 1:12-13, NIV).

GOD IS OUR LAPIDARY

Like precious gems, women of African ancestry are being cut, shaped, and polished into precious stones. In the colorful garden of jewels that make up the world of Black women, each of us endured great difficulty to become who and what we are. Many of us would love to be rich and famous like Oprah, a world leader like African humanitarian Graca Machel, an educator like Renita Weems, or an athletic champion like Venus or Serena Williams. We must understand that the same potential that causes Oprah, Graca, Renita, and the Williams sisters to shine so brightly resides in us. But are you willing to make the sacrifices that greatness calls for?

If you truly wish to reach your hidden potential, then look with me at three things that give jewels their value: *beauty, endurance,* and *rarity.*

Beauty. Each of us has something beautiful about us, even if it is hidden. We can either complain about feeling unattractive and unloved, or we can place ourselves in the hands of the Master lapidary and allow God to help us uncover and celebrate our own particular beauty. Like a fine jewel whose beauty comes from the deep facets within the stone that capture and reflect light, our beauty does not come from the surface. Perhaps that's what Jesus meant when he said: "Let your light so shine before [people], that they may see your good works and glorify your Father in heaven" (Matthew 5:16).

Endurance. To endure means to suffer but never surrender. Building endurance is difficult, yet it strengthens our character. Certain types of cutting and polishing can protect a jewel from being chipped and scratched from later wear and tear. Splendid athletes willingly submit themselves to pain and discipline in order to win. The Bible reads like a spiritual obstacle course as it directs us to endure persecution, slander, hardships, and suffering. God speaks to us through the book of Hebrews: "You have need of endurance, so that after you have done the will of God, you may receive the promise" (10:36).

Rarity. A person who has the courage to step away from the crowd and follow God's unique plan for her life is rare indeed. She is like a matchless jewel that is set apart from all others. Sometimes the cost of being "uncommon" is isolation and ridicule. Yet from this separation out of the world come rare solutions, rare courage, and rare faith. This rare jewel of a woman who is ahead of her time prepares her table with wisdom and knowledge for those who will one day search for the path that leads to her door. "Lips that speak knowledge are a rare jewel" (Proverbs 20:15, NIV).

The challenge for many Black women is our inability to recognize and define our own beauty, endurance, and rarity. As jewels, many of us have been falsely appraised, subjected to the sapphire stereotype and other labels that devalue our worth. I cannot count the times that I have listened to women of African descent recite a résumé of what they don't like about themselves: hair, skin color, body size, facial features. And just as often I hear, "Men don't want Black women." In the past, I shared those sentiments. But once I discovered that my true worth is clearly spelled out in the Word of God, I was no longer a slave to such perceptions. The Bible says: "I will praise You, for I am fearfully and wonderfully made; marvelous are Your works, and that my soul knows very well" (Psalm 139:14).

We are the workmanship of Jesus, the Master lapidary. Because Western culture, the media, and certain men devalue us doesn't mean we are worthless. "For we are His workmanship, created in Christ Jesus for good works, which God prepared beforehand that we should walk in them" (Ephesians 2:10).

Those who are careless, or who don't know the worth of what they have, often throw away valuables. I recently read an article on Dumpster diving. "Divers," as they are called, visit the back alley Dumpsters of hotels, office buildings, and retail stores in search of treasures. One diver reported that he often finds computers, printers, and other supplies that he cashes in for hundreds and sometimes thousands of dollars. Another diver found a Rolex watch that appraised for fifteen thousand dollars.

"[God] stoops to look, and lifts the poor from the dirt, and the hungry from the garbage dump, and sets them among princes[ses]!" (Psalm 113:6-8, TLB). You are so valuable to God that even though he is holy and pure, he comes down to the smelly, germ-infested garbage dump of this world and searches through the trash in hopes of reclaiming you. Wouldn't you do the same if you lost something of real value? If you owned a diamond ring and it fell into the trash, or even a toilet, would you not reach in hoping to retrieve it?

You may be going through a period in your life that makes you feel like you have been broken into pieces and thrown away. You may not be in a place where you have an opportunity to shine; you may have been left in the shadows. Perhaps the Master lapidary is not yet finished shaping and polishing you into a perfect jewel.

Whatever your condition or circumstance, God is not finished with you yet! Once the process of cutting and polishing is complete, then you are fully prepared to step into the perfect setting and design for your life where you will shine!

Being confident of this very thing,
that He who has begun a good work in you
will complete it until the day of Jesus Christ.

Philippians 1:6

Chapter 3

The Master Jeweler

Discovering God's Perfect Design

I made you grow like a plant of the field. You grew up and
developed and became the most beautiful of jewels.... I gave
you my solemn oath and entered into a covenant with you,
declares the Sovereign LORD, and you became mine.

EZEKIEL 16:7-8, NIV

Like an artistic jewelry designer who selects the perfect setting for a beautiful gem, God—who formed you, then shaped and polished you—has already prepared the perfect setting and design for your life. The Lord's plan will bring you fulfillment while bringing glory and honor to his name.

Where you find yourself is not an accident; it is God's perfect plan. Bessie Head was born in a South African mental asylum to a psychotic mother, yet she became one of South Africa's most famous authors. The circumstance of your birth has nothing to do with your destiny. Racism, poverty, and gender do not determine our course in life. God alone controls the future, as illustrated by these words from the book of Isaiah: "I make known the end from the beginning, from ancient times, what is still

to come. I say: My purpose will stand, and I will do all that I please"
(Isaiah 46:10, NIV).

The story of Mansa, a Caribbean master jeweler, reveals much about
God as well as the design and setting he has for our lives.

Mansa carefully enters the code to deactivate the burglar alarm and opens
the heavy brass and mahogany doors to his elegant jewelry store. The echo
of his footsteps on the polished marble floor fades as he enters the vault
where he keeps his precious stones, filed away in rows of metal drawers.

It is early morning and the hot Caribbean sun does not yet glare
through Mansa's beautiful display windows, nor have the tourists from the
luxury hotels nearby begun shopping. Mansa's daily ritual is to spend several quiet hours in his design shop making art from his array of sparkling
jewels. The lapidary gives precious stones their form and structure; Mansa
designs their destiny. He is the craftsman who transforms gems into the
jewelry that has meaning and significance.

A solitary diamond ring in a raised platinum setting signifies the
promise of love and marriage. A string of delicate pearls is a gift a mother
presents to her daughter on her graduation day, the clasp bearing the girl's
initials in sterling silver. A dark emerald stone in a massive gold setting of
eagle's wings will adorn the hand of a champion athlete.

Guided by the Master of all creation, Mansa pours himself into each
creation. Then he places his pieces of delicate art in the display window on
a plush velvet platform and waits for the day they will fulfill their destiny.

Like other craftsmen of fine jewels, Mansa enjoys the company of precious stones and often converses with them. Jewels can be very tempera-
mental because of their great beauty, and Mansa faces many challenges in

transforming them into meaningful works of art. Sometimes a precious jewel has one design in mind, while Mansa has a totally different plan.

Pearl, for example, is fairly large with a unique shape. Her great ambition was to be strung onto a long necklace with her loved ones. Mansa, however, set her in a solitary ring with a white gold setting, surrounded with diamonds.

"I can't stand diamonds!" Pearl argued with Mansa. "I don't want to be with a bunch of snooty diamonds. They think they're better than me!"

Mansa was calm. "But you are the centerpiece," he tried to explain. "The diamonds only serve to make you look even more beautiful."

Pearl was unhappy and disappointed when she found herself stuck in a situation that went against her hopes and dreams. Of course Mansa tried to explain to her that a string of pearls must all be the same size, shape, and color. Pearl simply wouldn't fit in. His plan was not to hide but to highlight Pearl's special beauty and thereby increase her value.

Likewise, the Lord says to us: "'For I know the plans I have for you,' declares the LORD, 'plans to prosper you and not to harm you, plans to give you hope and a future'" (Jeremiah 29:11, NIV).

When you are locked into a certain way of thinking, it is hard for God, as the Master jeweler, to achieve his perfect design for your life. Too many Black women look in the mirror and don't like what they see. We often spend our time comparing ourselves to a standard of beauty that does not include women of African ancestry. The Bible says in Genesis 1:31 that everything God created is "very good." In spite of how you see yourself, you are perfectly designed for God's purpose.

Diamond is another of Mansa's precious jewels. A flawless five-carat stone, she does not understand why she is constantly overlooked. Mansa has given her the best place in the display case. Everyone wants to hold her, touch her; but she is always placed back in the case while a smaller stone, in a less dramatic setting is placed in a velvet box and carried away. On the outside Diamond remains composed, but on the inside she harbors the secret pain of feeling rejected and unloved.

"You are more desirable than all the rest," Mansa reassures her, "but not many people can afford a jewel of your quality. So you must patiently wait, just as you did when you rested quietly in the earth. Your day will come!"

"Something must be wrong with me," Black women lament. My response: Something is so right with you that the average person just can't handle it. Imagine the five-carat Diamond saying to Mansa, "Cut me in half and scratch me a little so someone will want me." Yet many Black women find ways to devalue their own worth.

Mansa also spends time with one of his most fragile yet beautiful jewels, Opal. She is a rare black opal who has been placed in a rich gold pendant to be worn as a necklace. When Opal is in the light, she instantly comes alive with a prism of colors that illuminate the depths of her loveliness. People are in awe of her structure and versatility. Opal loves the light and doesn't understand why Mansa is so overly protective and keeps her in a cool, quiet place. How she would love to sit in the display window day in and day out, enjoying the admiration of those who pass by and come inside to shop. She could stay in the light forever, but Mansa knows better. Constant bright light might cause Opal to become brittle and even crack. Even when customers come into the shop to inquire about Opal, Mansa rarely allows her to be handled.

"But why can't I be out there like the others? They are loved, touched, handled, and admired," Opal argues.

We may not understand why God keeps us out of the spotlight or why doors of opportunity seem to remain closed. But the Word tells us that "all things work together for good to those who love God, to those who are the called according to His purpose" (Romans 8:28).

Often the Lord withholds our greatest desires to protect us from what he knows will do more harm than good. I imagine the complaints that tennis champions Venus and Serena Williams must have made as little girls living in the middle of gang-ridden Compton, California. "Why can't we go out with our friends? Why can't we be like other kids?" I am sure they understand now that their lives were being carefully orchestrated for greatness.

Women of other races appear in the spotlight, getting all the glory. It is amazing how our culture celebrates anorexic fashion models and entertainers who have been completely altered by plastic surgery. Some will perform any ungodly act for acceptance, and the price of fame is more than any woman should be asked to pay. Many young Black women are embracing these beauty standards and destructive lifestyles. The Lord weeps as his precious jewels cast themselves before swine.

Mansa, the master jeweler, understands the struggles of all types of jewels. One of his most prized possessions is Ruby. Their first meeting was a strange encounter. One night, just before closing, a man came into Mansa's shop hoping to sell a tarnished ring with a dull red stone. "I'll take whatever you give me," the man pleaded. Mansa carefully examined the stone and couldn't believe his eyes. Ruby was a rare, flawless jewel that had been badly mistreated. He gave the nervous man a few dollars and watched as he hurried down the street.

"How did you come into that man's possession?" Mansa spoke gently to the stone as she lay on his worktable.

"It's a long and terrible story," Ruby whispered.

Mansa polished Ruby as much as he could, but her glow still lacked the true luster of a jewel of her stature. "Why are you working so hard on me? Can't you see that I'm not worth anything?" Ruby said sadly.

Suddenly, Mansa realized what was wrong with Ruby. She was filled with insecurities because she didn't recognize her true worth. Little did she know that an authentic ruby of her quality is one of the most rare and sought-after jewels on earth.

Mansa spoke gently to this precious jewel. "Most red stones are only masquerading as rubies, but you, my dear Ruby, are the real thing. You are not just another red stone—you are an authentic, priceless jewel."

Day after day Mansa reminded Ruby of her worth and beauty. As Ruby pondered his words, her insecurities slowly vanished. One day she straightened herself and released a fiery radiance that could only come from the heart of a jewel of her magnitude. She would never again see herself as a worthless red stone.

DISCOVERING GOD'S PERFECT PLAN

Our challenge as Black women is to allow ourselves to be transformed from rough gemstones into polished jewels, designed by the Master. Three important characteristics are necessary to allow the beauty God has placed within you to be revealed and celebrated:

1. Vision. A vision is God allowing you to see the plan and purpose that lies beyond your present condition. To know your true identity and purpose, you must allow God to open your spiritual eyes. If you spend time in prayer and in the Word of God, his plan for your life will begin to unfold. The Lord will never show you anything you are not capable of achieving. His design for you is flawless, and when the design has been fully realized, your untapped beauty will be fully revealed.

2. Faith. Have faith that God will lead you into the purpose for which you were created. Walking in faith takes courage, especially when you can't see how God is going to work things out. Rather than dwell on the big picture—how you will pay for school, move to the next level in your career, start a ministry or business—take one step at a time. Apply for school or write down your ministry or business plan, then allow God to show you what to do next. Where he guides, he provides. True beauty radiates from the woman who reaches out in faith to achieve her greatest dream.

3. Perseverance. Whatever you hope to achieve in life will take courage and perseverance. Prayer is the only thing that can build perseverance. Prayer gives you the willingness to fight, suffer, sacrifice, discipline yourself, and endure hardships. It is one thing to have a dream and a vision, but it will take perseverance to make your dream a reality. Talented people reach their goals, not because they are talented, but because they are willing to make the sacrifice that greatness requires.

Let me encourage you to make the following confessions each day, which will stand as a constant reminder to you that your heavenly Father is shaping and designing you into a beautiful jewel:

I am not an accident. I am a perfect design.

I am God's creation. His plan for me is perfect.

I am valuable, no matter what my circumstances.

King David, the psalmist, discovered that even before he was born, all the days of his life were already planned by the Lord.

> *Your eyes saw my substance, being yet unformed.*
> *And in Your book they all were written,*
> *The days fashioned for me,*
> *When as yet there were none of them.*
>
> PSALM 139:16

Chapter 4

Twelve Beautiful Jewels

Identifying and Accepting Your Gifts

They fashioned the breastpiece—the work of skilled craftsman....
Then they mounted four rows of precious stones on it. In the first
row there was a ruby, a topaz and a beryl; in the second row a
turquoise, a sapphire and an emerald; in the third row a jacinth,
an agate and an amethyst; in the fourth row a chrysolite, an
onyx and a jasper. They were mounted in gold filigree settings.

EXODUS 39:8,10-13, NIV

Exodus tells the story of how God used Moses to lead the children of
Israel out of bondage in Egypt. No other book in the Bible parallels the
struggle of Black people like this Old Testament writing.

You may remember that God commanded Moses to build a taber-
nacle in the wilderness and to make a special garment for Aaron the high
priest. God also divinely commissioned a stonecutter to make a breastplate
for the high priest to wear (see Exodus 31:2-10). It would be covered with
twelve different jewels, each representing one of the twelve tribes of Israel,
the descendants of the patriarch Jacob and his twelve sons (see 39:14).

The face of each jewel was engraved with the name of the tribe it represented, showing that God's love for each of the tribes of Israel was permanently engraved upon his heart. Now that you know what goes into the making of a jewel, you can appreciate the Lord's use of jewels for his divine purpose. The twelve tribes were as precious and beautiful as twelve shining jewels in the sight of God. "See, I have engraved you on the palms of my hands" (Isaiah 49:16, NIV).

It is significant that the Lord used jewels to symbolize his love for each of the tribes, but it is also important to note that God used different types of jewels. Each had a unique type of beauty that set it apart from the others. Just as jewels are different in their appearance and makeup, so were the personalities of the twelve sons of Jacob. Similarly, women of African descent are created with different colors, sizes, shapes, and personalities, yet they are all beautiful in their own way.

The jewels of the high priest's breastplate are identified in Exodus 28:17-20 and 39:10-13. Archaeologists and scholars are not fully certain which tribes were associated with which jewels in Aaron's breastplate, and over the last three thousand years, names of the jewels have changed. However, the following summary shows the view many scholars share about which jewels might have been associated with the specific twelve tribes of Israel.

JEWEL	NAME	MEANING
Ruby	Judah	Praise
Topaz	Issachar	Reward
Beryl	Zebulun	Dwelling Place
Turquoise	Reuben	Behold a Son
Sapphire	Simeon	God Hears

JEWEL	NAME	MEANING
Diamond	Gad	Good Fortune
Opal	Ephraim	Double Fruitful
Agate	Manasseh	Causing to Forget
Amethyst	Benjamin	Right-Hand Son
Emerald	Dan	Good Judgment
Onyx	Asher	Blessed
Pearl*	Naphtali	Wrestle

In African and Middle Eastern culture, a name represented the nature of a person or a circumstance surrounding their birth. As you can tell from the list, the twelve tribes demonstrated a wide range of personality types. One of the names means "praise." Another name means "good judgment," and another means "double fruitful." When the tribes of Israel were later scattered throughout the earth, they remained spiritually joined together, like the twelve jewels on Aaron's breastplate.

Their story is not unlike that of people of African ancestry around the world. I grew up in a church in Philadelphia where the women sang gospel songs, with a vibrant soprano or a rich alto leading the chorus and the other women responding to the chant. They waved their handkerchiefs and sometimes shouted and danced when the Spirit was high. When the time of thanksgiving and praise ended, the women would fan themselves and settle down to listen to the sermon.

My first worship service in the Caribbean Islands felt like I was still in Philadelphia. None of the women had ever been to America, and I had never before been to the Caribbean Islands, but to my amazement, they

---

* possibly jasper

sang, danced, and worshiped just like the women of my home church. My experience was similar on a trip to Africa; I found the languages were different, but the worship was always the same: dancing, waving white handkerchiefs, and chanting praises to the Lord.

The women traveling with me all wept when we realized that after hundreds of years of separation from our heritage by slavery, Black women continue to share the same sisterhood. We have been scattered around the world, yet we remain joined together like precious jewels in a breastplate of love and spiritual unity.

Like fine jewels, we have different kinds of inner and outer beauty. In the next few chapters I will explore twelve different types of Black women. All of them will be compared to a particular jewel from the high priest's breastplate.

As you read, I hope you will gain a better insight into the following facets of a Black woman's character:

Strength. This is usually defined as the ability to exercise force and to endure adversity. In the records of African history, strength can also be seen in patient resolve and steadfastness in circumstances that, for many, never changed. Our ancestors who lived through slavery and discrimination were sustained by a supernatural strength. We will explore the mystery of the natural and spiritual strength of Black women.

Weakness. We all have weaknesses, but they can be overcome when addressed properly. The following chapters will not condemn you for having weaknesses nor help you find excuses for your behavior, but they will show you ways to triumph over weaknesses and provide building materials to strengthen and fortify you where you need wholeness.

Self-esteem. How you treat yourself will determine how others treat you. I pray that you will discover your real value by recognizing your particular type of beauty, purpose, talent, and anointing. When you begin to agree with God that you are "all that," you will begin to treat yourself with a new level of love and respect and separate yourself from any lifestyle or person that devalues you.

Confidence. Each of us must find the courage to risk because we believe in ourselves. My desire is that as you develop a new sense of "God-confidence," you will also develop a new level of self-confidence. Perhaps there are things you don't like about your "self." Consider that they may be the very attributes God intended to be your special gift. Remember, God said that everything he made was "very good" (Genesis 1:31).

Anointing. This involves a release of God's power on a person for a specific area of service. It is to aid in the calling that God has for your life. Spiritual maturity is critical if you want your anointing to be a blessing and not a curse to your calling. I will help you to recognize your anointing and then to fully live and use your gifting from God. I hope to help you learn to trust God in a deeper way.

Talent. Worth more than silver and gold, the talent given to each of us by God causes our beauty to shine and brings us true success. Saying you have no talent simply means that you have not yet discovered your talent. It is your responsibility to search for it like hidden treasure. You may also need to overcome your fears and insecurities to release your talents. Some women have so many talents they don't know how to harness what God has given them. Master your talents one at a time because different talents are given to you for different seasons in your life.

If you keep these six facets in mind as you explore the following descriptions of twelve types of women of African ancestry, I believe that in one of these jewels you will find the mirrored image of your own beauty. I pray that the Holy Spirit will help you enhance and even redefine your self-image by allowing you to discover new and exciting dimensions of yourself. My desire is also that the following pages will enable you to help other women in your life discover their special anointing or talents and become more fulfilled. This is the role of a true spiritual sister.

As the mystery of your creation continues to unfold, may you be like a joyful psalmist, writing and singing words to a melody that expresses how the grace and glory of God has made you beautiful.

O LORD, you have searched me
and you know me.
You know when I sit and when I rise;
you perceive my thoughts from afar....
Such knowledge is too wonderful for me,
too lofty for me to attain.

PSALM 139:1-2,6, NIV

Chapter 5

The Beauty of Ruby

A Woman of Virtue and Praise

Who can find a virtuous woman? for her price is far above rubies.

PROVERBS 31:10, KJV

We read in Exodus 28:17 that the ruby was the first stone to be placed on Aaron's breastplate. Scholars believe that this stone represented the tribe of Judah, whose name means "praise."

As the fourth son of Jacob and Leah, Judah is the most significant of all the tribes because it is the lineage of King David, a man of praise. More important, Jesus Christ was a direct descendant of the tribe of Judah. That is why our Lord is often referred to as the Lion of Judah.

Although Judah's placement as first came as a result of the moral failures of his older brothers, all things do work together for good because praise comes first with God. The fiery red ruby makes a perfect symbol for the passionate praise and worship that ushers us into the presence of the Lord, where every petition written in our hearts is clearly discerned.

In addition to being a symbol of praise, the ruby is noted in Proverbs 31:10 as a point of comparison for a virtuous woman. Like a precious ruby, the virtuous woman is the product of time, heat, and pressure. God has given her the strength to keep standing through hard times. Her faith has been tested and forged in the heat of adversity, and when the pressure is on, instead of breaking, her passionate red flame shines more brightly than ever.

Most of us think of a virtuous woman as one who is celebrated for her moral excellence. But in the full spectrum of a virtuous woman, we must include not only moral excellence but also spiritual excellence, which is demonstrated by inner strength, healing virtue, courage, and valor. Like the rare ruby buried deep in the earth, virtue (which translates into power within your soul) can only be discovered and released when you follow the treasure map of righteousness and obedience that is found in the Word of God. Praise ushers us into the presence of God, but virtuous living ushers us into the power of God.

In a culture where righteousness and godliness have been devalued, while wickedness and immorality are encouraged and even celebrated, it takes strength and courage for a virtuous woman to stand for what is right. She may not openly condemn others for their lifestyles, but she makes no apologies for choosing to reject any practice that opposes the Word of God.

A life of praise and intimacy with Christ gives the virtuous woman the strength and courage to live in moral excellence. Obedience to God's standard of holiness is more valuable in his sight than the most precious rubies of this world.

The ruby is often called the Lord of the Gems because of its rarity and beauty. It is a well-known fact among jewelers that many red stones sold as rubies are not rubies at all. Less valuable gems are sometimes chemically transformed to a deep ruby-red color. Another common practice is to use a high degree of heat to affix a layer of ground ruby to the surface of a less valuable gem. But true rubies, second only to diamonds in strength and value, are among the most rare and costly jewels in the world.

As a Black woman who possesses the characteristics of a true ruby, you are a precious and valuable gift in the sight of God. You allow the people around you to draw from your strength and virtue. You are not easily intimidated, and you are not afraid to set a standard of godliness for other women to follow.

You often find yourself in the company of women who are similar to imitation rubies. They seem to possess spiritual power, but closer inspection exposes it as a substitute. They raise their hands in praise and adoration. They pray beautiful prayers, but the results never come. They go through all the motions in order to reach God, but they are like a person trying to start a fire with a book of matches and a stack of wet wood. They might eventually cause a little flicker to appear, but it quickly fades. As a Black woman who is a true ruby, you are a fire starter, because the fire is within you.

The man in your life is especially blessed because he knows he can trust you with his whole heart (see Proverbs 31:11). With you as a passionate intercessor, he lacks nothing in his life. You know how to cover your loved ones with winged prayers that fly into the very presence of the Lord.

As a woman of virtue, you have experienced pain, yet because of your passionate relationship with the Lord, your pain has been turned into power. Just the thought of what God has brought you through causes the flames of praise to leap into the heavens. You engulf everyone around you with an attitude of gratitude. Because you possess the virtue of a flaming ruby, don't be surprised when other women come to you seeking prayer, wise counsel, and encouragement. Continue to replenish your power with a life of praise and obedience to God.

The air is filled with a dry, stifling heat. A cloud of dust ascends into a swirling funnel as the crowds of people run along the road and press in to catch a glimpse of—and hopefully even to touch—the stranger from Galilee. Rumors in the streets and marketplace recount that with a word or a touch, this man called Jesus can heal the sick and even raise the dead. His power to heal and cast out demons has been confirmed as families rejoice because their loved ones have been restored to wholeness.

A thin, sickly woman who has suffered with menstrual bleeding for twelve years covers her face with her cloak to keep the choking dust out of her throat as well as to hide her identity. In her time and culture, it is unlawful for a menstruating woman to enter a public place. But the woman has run out of choices just as she has run out of doctors and the money to pay for their treatments. She no longer feels decent and acceptable. She has lost her sense of beauty, her self-esteem, and the simple joy of being a woman. She has come to a place where she needs to experience God's power, not religious ritual.

Earlier in the day she'd been crying and singing praises to the Lord. The praises began as a desperate attempt to drown out the voices of doubt and discouragement that tried to tell her that if God was real, then surely he would not have allowed her to suffer all these years. On this particular day, the voices were louder than they had ever been. They urged her to bring her suffering to an end by taking her own life. The woman put her hands over her ears and sang as loudly as she could, praising the Lord. It was the only way to drown out the terrible voices.

Then without understanding how she gained the courage and strength to leave her house, the woman found herself walking on the crowded street. It was as though some unseen force was leading her. For a moment she felt faint, but a new surge of strength filled her body as she pressed onward to an unknown destination.

"Jesus is coming!" a boy shouts, nearly knocking the woman over as he hurries down the street.

"Heal us, Lord. Please heal us!" People are pleading from the swelling crowd. The woman is caught in the press. She tries to push forward, but she is like a small piece of driftwood swirling on a rushing tide. Suddenly, everything stands still as the woman catches a glimpse of Jesus passing on the road. With one last burst of strength she presses through the crowd and reaches out to touch him.

"Lord! Have mercy on me!" she cries out as she grabs the hem of his dusty robe. A surge of power grips every part of her being. She gags her mouth with her dress to keep from crying out with joy, for she knows the sickness is gone and will never return.

Jesus stops in his tracks. His piercing eyes run to and fro as the crowd continues to press in against the restraining arms of the disciples. "Somebody touched me!" Jesus said. "For I perceive that virtue is gone out of me."

The woman trembles with fear, imagining an awful fate might follow such a presumptuous act. But as she lifts her eyes she can see Jesus looking back at her. His smile and gentle gaze dissolves all of her apprehension.

"Daughter, don't be afraid. Your faith has made you well. Go in peace."

The preceding story is adapted from Luke 8, where we learn that from faith comes healing virtue. Some Bible translations use the word *power* in the place of *virtue,* but the meaning is unchanged. The virtue that came from Jesus had the power to completely heal the sick woman.

Similarly, a virtuous woman has a healing effect on people who are broken and bruised. She stirs up faith in the people around her, and women are able to press through their issues because of her love and encouragement.

There can be no better way to describe the beauty of a Black woman who is both spiritually powerful and morally excellent than to say she is like a precious ruby. In making this comparison, let's consider three types of rare rubies: the star ruby, the Burmese ruby, and the Mong Hsu ruby.

THE STAR RUBY

Unlike the transparent flame of the traditional red ruby, the extremely rare star ruby is a silky smooth rounded stone. Under the light it reflects a six-point star that looks like long crystal needles. The star (an effect known as "asterism") emanates from the center of the stone. The only equal to the star ruby is her sister jewel, the star sapphire. (Rubies and sapphires share the same physical properties but are distinguished by the difference in color.)

Both the star ruby and the virtuous Black woman are brilliant and unique. In the life of a ruby woman, the six points that emanate from the star ruby stand as a reminder of six (of the nine) spiritual gifts listed in 1 Corinthians 12: wisdom, knowledge, faith, healing, miracles, and discernment. One or more of these spiritual gifts is bestowed upon every believer in Christ to empower them to fulfill God's purpose (see verse 11).

Wisdom is the spiritual gift that shows us how to apply the knowledge of God to our daily lives. Scripture often associates wisdom with rubies. Job 28:18 states, "The price of wisdom is above rubies." With all of its beauty, the star ruby has only material value, but the woman who possesses the gift of wisdom has been given the keys to long life, riches, and honor (see Proverbs 3:16). A woman of virtue spends time in the

Bible and other books that are filled with wisdom. She seeks the counsel of wise men and women, and because of her pursuits she adds to her wisdom and shines brighter than a star ruby.

Knowledge involves acquiring information and skills that help us overcome adversity and fulfill our maximum potential. Proverbs 20:15 reads, "Lips that speak knowledge are a rare jewel" (NIV). A woman of virtue understands that acquiring knowledge is a lifelong pursuit. She recognizes that she is never too young or too old to gain new information and new skills. Such achievements help the virtuous woman reach higher levels of confidence and increase her value.

Faith is a spiritual gift that allows the woman of virtue to look beyond the visible realm and see the plan, possibilities, and promises that can only be seen with the eyes of the spirit. Isaiah 7:9 tells us, "If you do not stand firm in your faith, you will not stand at all" (NIV). A woman of virtue stands firm on the promises of God. She may have her moments of discouragement, but a season of praise renews her strength, and she presses forward to receive the reward that comes with great faith.

Healing is an awesome gift that can bring wholeness not only to the mind, emotions, and body of one person but to entire families, communities, and nations. The woman of virtue anchors herself in faith and ministers prayers of healing, recognizing that wholeness can come only when the virtue of Jesus Christ is released into the lives of those who believe in his name. "For there went virtue out of [Jesus], and healed them all" (Luke 6:19, KJV).

Miracles are occurrences that defy the limits of human ability and possibilities. For the Black woman who lives a life of virtue, miracles are often a way of life. When facing great obstacles, the virtuous woman of color is accustomed to seeing God respond to her prayers with miracles. It is a spiritual gift that calls for complete dependence on God's mercy and grace. Some are prophets. Some are teachers. Others work miracles. (See 1 Corinthians 12:28.)

Discernment is the gift of correct judgment based on spiritual insight. The virtuous woman clearly demonstrates the gift of discernment. Because of her intimacy with the Lord, her spirit is like a radar screen that can easily make a clear judgment between good and evil. Those who are mature can "discern both good and evil" (Hebrews 5:14).

BURMESE RUBY

This celebrated jewel, known for its vivid red color, is marked by a dark blue core resembling a fiery blue flame. Because of the deep richness of its color, it is sometimes called "pigeon's blood" or "dove's blood."

In several passages of the Bible, the dove is mentioned as the gentle bird that was brought to the temple to be sacrificed on the altar. The dove was offered only by the poor and downtrodden among the Jews, while the wealthy and prominent presented a lamb or bull to be sacrificed (see Leviticus 12:8).

In Middle Eastern culture the dove has very little material value, but it is rich in spiritual symbolism. The dove signifies peace, gentleness, sacrifice, and even the presence of the Holy Spirit. Solomon used the vivid imagery of the dove as he wrote of a beautiful, nameless woman he called the Shulamite.

He describes her skin as dark, like the tents of Kedar (see Song of Solomon 1:5). In Middle Eastern and North African culture, women who lived in poverty often worked outdoors in the fields chopping grain or picking fruit. Sunburned skin, like the tents of Kedar, was considered a mark of poverty or a lower social station.

Whatever the Shulamite's social status or coloring, Solomon (who is a poetic symbol of Christ in this passage) finds this dark and lovely woman to be beautiful and irresistible. Solomon celebrates her in 4:1: "Behold, you are fair, my love!… You have dove's eyes behind your veil." The Shulamite had the eyes of a woman who was innocent, without guilt. Perhaps he also likened her to a powerless bird in a world of winged predators.

As the passage continues, King Solomon lovingly pours out words of affirmation that would make any woman feel like a flawless, precious jewel: "All beautiful you are, my darling; there is no flaw in you" (4:7, NIV). Over and over he spares no words in helping the Shulamite see that she is much more than a dove whose only value was to be offered up as a meager sacrifice. Her neck is beautiful "with strings of jewels," Solomon declares (1:10, NIV).

If the Shulamite was undervalued by others or herself, King Solomon had another perception of her. He was the ultimate judge of beauty and perfection, and in essence, he boldly declared that the woman was more precious than a dove-blood ruby. Without a doubt his appraisal came directly from the heart of God: "my darling, my dove, my flawless one" (5:2, NIV).

The precious value of the "dove's blood" (or Burmese) ruby brings to mind the sacrifices of so many African women. I am grateful for all of the virtuous Black women of the past who were like loving doves, sacrificing their very blood for the lives of others without seeking any recognition or reward.

For many women the word *sacrifice* brings to mind images of miserable self-denial or giving your all in order to gain a few crumbs of acceptance or approval. But real sacrifice is a much higher calling. It is the essence of true virtue because sacrifice happens when one person joyfully gives up what she cherishes and values to express love and commitment to another. There are no strings attached and no expectation of being appreciated, accepted, or loved in return. "For God so loved the world that He gave His only begotten Son" (John 3:16). Like the blood of an innocent dove, the ruby-red blood of Jesus was shed on Calvary's cross as an expression of his love for us.

Sacrifice is as pure and joyful as a kindergarten child who passionately cuts out a red heart and painstakingly pastes it to a piece of white paper. Then with a big red crayon, she writes the words *I love you.* When the gift is given, there is no feeling of misery or self-denial—it is all joy. When you look at the beauty of a ruby, allow it to remind you of the joyful sacrifices that Christ made for you. As you give thanks for all that was given on your behalf, purpose in your heart to demonstrate godly virtue by willingly sacrificing for others.

MONG HSU RUBY

When this unique ruby was first discovered, it was believed to hold very little value as a precious jewel. The core of the stone had a dark center surrounded by a bright red rim. No one wanted this stone with a dark, flawed core until a gemologist made a wonderful discovery. When the Mong Hsu ruby was placed in a hot fire, the dark core disappeared, leaving behind a brilliant red ruby. Because of this process, much like purging, the value of the ruby has been completely restored.

In a spiritual sense, purging is the painful process that empties us of sin and leads to repentance. This process may include loss, disappointment, and tough consequences for our actions. The thing that we once found attractive becomes grotesque. What once brought pleasure becomes too painful to bear. God allows us to suffer in the furnace of transformation until he hears us say in our heart, "Never again!" Like a Mong Hsu ruby placed in a fire, the stain of sin at the core of our soul disappears, allowing our true beauty to shine through. This experience is a type of sanctification.

Sanctification is the process of learning how to maintain our purity and holiness in the sight of God. By doing so, we live a joyful life of praise and power. Praise opens the floodgates of power. Virtuous living turns our souls and spirits into vessels in which the power of God is stored.

Once you have been filled with the power of God, you must beware of leaks caused by sin. Sin will reduce and even empty you of God's power. Sanctification, which translates into separating yourself from the lifestyle and values of your culture, must be maintained if you expect to walk in the fullness of God's power and authority.

Like the Mong Hsu ruby, every believer must be purified by fire in order to tap into the depths of God's power. "Before I was afflicted I went astray, but now I keep Your word" (Psalm 119:67).

Here are five important steps to maintaining purity, praise, and virtue:

1. Say no to sinful practices. When we participate in things that are not pleasing to God, it puts a blemish on our soul and robs us of our beauty. More and more I see young women who look old and worn because of sinful practices. Sin not only drains your outer beauty, it also drains you of spiritual power and blocks your access to God. Satan is constantly searching for ways to rob you of spiritual power so that when you are faced with a challenge you will not be able to handle the difficulty. "She who hates virtue is covered with shame" (Proverbs 11:16, NRSV).

2. Make forgiveness a daily exercise. Each day, confess any thoughts and behaviors that are not pleasing to God, and forgive those who have wounded you. Holding on to unforgiveness not only robs you of access to God, it also robs you of your health, your physical and spiritual beauty, and your peace of mind. It is like having a hole in the gas tank of your car. No matter how many times you fill up, the power leaks out because you have not repaired broken relationships. Without forgiveness you cannot experience the power of God in your life. Forgive as the Lord forgave you (see Colossians 3:13).

3. Practice being quiet. Turn off the television, radio, pager, fax, computer, music, and even people who block your signal into heavenly places. "Quiet" welcomes the presence of God and allows you to clearly hear his voice. First Peter 3:3-4 states that beauty should not come from the clothes we wear but from the unfading beauty of a gentle and quiet spirit. A quiet spirit can only be obtained when you spend time in prayer and meditation. As you meditate on God's Word, He will empower you and renew you. "I will meditate on Your precepts, and contemplate Your ways" (Psalm 119:15).

4. Make praising God a creative experience. Find your own personal way to tell God how much you love him. I personally like to walk in the mountains near my house several times a week. Even when it's raining, I like to climb the mountain trails and watch the birds, deer, and other animals. Some people would rather write in a prayer journal or sing to the Lord. Celebrate God in a manner that fits your personality and leaves you feeling beautiful and spiritually refreshed. "Praise the LORD!… For it is pleasant, and praise is beautiful" (Psalm 147:1).

5. Count your blessings. Nothing blesses the Lord more than an attitude of gratitude. As you praise the Lord in all things, the Holy Spirit will fill you with renewed strength and power. It is also important to recognize that what you may perceive as a problem can be a blessing in disguise. Give thanks in all things, no matter what you're going through. Satan is terrified of the weapon of praise because it is a major attack against the demons of failure and lack. Praise is a powerful weapon against Satan's kingdom. "Let the high praises of God be in [your] mouth, and a two-edged sword in [your] hand" (Psalm 149:6).

Ruby was the first to walk into the chilly sanctuary for morning prayer. Her body was tired, and the trouble in her family was enough to call up the National Guard. Even though she loved to gather with the members of the church for a time of praise and intercessory prayer, she was glad for the quietness and the absence of chatter and small talk before the time of prayer was officially called to order. Ruby fell on her knees and bowed her head. Tears welled in her eyes as her smooth alto voice softly rang out and traveled upward to heaven, where the holy angels bow before the throne of God.

"It's Ruby. She's entering into the presence of God," whispered an angel who was near the throne.

"What is her need?" another angel asked.

"It's never what she needs; it's always the needs of others," the first angel answered.

Suddenly their conversation was drowned out by Ruby's voice of praise: "With all of my heart…all of my soul…all of my mind…I love you, Lord. You are my strength, you are my fortress, you are my great deliverer. I've lost count of your blessings. There are no words to tell of your mercy. You are my friend, my champion, my present help…rest for my soul. Lord, teach me to love you more, to be faithful and true in all my ways."

The Lord stood to his feet and smiled. "Give her all that her heart desires," his voice rumbled throughout the heavens.

One of the angels who had recently been assigned to a place of worship at the throne of God looked perplexed. "But she has not asked for anything. She has only come to give you praise," he blurted out.

God smiled at the angel. "And I will reward the praise that she has freely given. I know all that she carries in her heart, and I will grant every unspoken petition. She has a husband who has strayed away from me. I will gently guide him back. A woman in her prayer group is very sick. I will put my healing in Ruby's touch. Someone in Ruby's family is struggling with addiction. Another is discouraged and about to give up on life. I will put my words of encouragement in Ruby's mouth. The more Ruby praises me and lives a life of virtue before me, the more I will fill her with my power."

Ruby's personal time with the Lord came to a close, and she suddenly became aware of the people who had come into the sanctuary and were crying out in prayer. Her tiredness was completely gone, and she felt as light as a feather. She whispered a quiet prayer and laid her hand on a member of her prayer group who had been stricken with cancer and was in terrible pain. No one noticed when Ruby picked up her Bible and purse and left the sanctuary. They were too busy rejoicing over the woman who was shouting that her pain was gone and that she could feel strength returning to her body.

Ruby walked out into the cold morning air. She raised her hands and gave thanks to God for his goodness. That's the way it's always been with Ruby; she stays in the background living a life that pleases the Lord, quietly giving him praise and glory with a fiery passion that can only come from a true Ruby.

Praise the LORD!
For it is good to sing praises to our God;
For it is pleasant, and praise is beautiful.

PSALM 147:1

Chapter 6

The Beauty of Topaz

A Woman of Vision and Reward

Give her the reward she has earned,
and let her works bring her praise at the city gate.

PROVERBS 31:31, NIV

Topaz, the second jewel mounted on Aaron's breastplate, is inscribed with the name Issachar, which means "wages" or "reward." Scripture also associates the name Issachar with one who has vision and understanding: "Of the sons of Issachar who had understanding of the times, to know what Israel ought to do, their chiefs were two hundred" (1 Chronicles 12:32).

In ancient days, the Egyptians viewed the golden topaz as a symbol of endurance. Vision coupled with endurance always leads to reward, whereas the Bible tells us that "where there is no vision, the people perish" (Proverbs 29:18, KJV).

So many signs indicate that our world is in serious trouble, yet the media and many Christian leaders act as if the rise of disease, the breakdown of families, fragile economies, and global conflicts are the norm. They are like Nero who played his fiddle while Rome burned.

Others, people with vision, are searching for answers and trying to figure out what to do.

The confusion and uncertainty of our times requires godly topaz women who, like the sons of Issachar, understand the times and know what to do. A woman of vision can be used by the Lord to keep her people from perishing.

My dear friend Bunny Wilson is serious about being prepared to face whatever difficulties might arise. We both live in Southern California, where earthquakes are a fact of life. After the Northridge earthquake hit California in 1994, bottled water that normally sold for two dollars was being sold for twenty dollars a bottle. Food was even harder to come by. Many of my friends camped out in their backyards because looters were breaking into homes with broken windows and doors.

Bunny wanted to be prepared in case the next "big one" should hit. This insightful woman took a short course in disaster training and then proceeded to store water underground. She created an emergency food storage unit complete with blankets, clothing, and first-aid supplies. She even called a neighborhood meeting and persuaded her entire block to become united in their efforts to protect their families in case of a disaster.

"What would you do if an earthquake hits and there's no electricity?" Bunny asked me.

"I'd light a candle," I answered.

Bunny shook her head indicating a wrong answer. "Never light a candle, because there might be a gas leak. Keep a flashlight by your bed and one in your car."

At first, I ignored what I thought were extreme actions on Bunny's part. But after giving the matter some thought, I recognized her insight. Following her advice I learned how to properly prepare for a disaster, because without a vision people perish.

Whether it is an earthquake or a terrorist attack, don't let the enemy catch you unprepared. Stock up on bottled water, dry goods, and emergency supplies. Don't let that day catch you unaware (see Luke 21:34).

The topaz woman carries the spirit of Issachar. She discerns the times and will always be rewarded for her vision and understanding. The man in her life will receive a full reward with this discerning woman by his side. Because she has her eye on the future and understands how to prepare for it, together they will always be one step ahead as they journey through life.

Despite the value of a vision, sometimes it will be rejected and scorned. In 1962, forty-five-year-old Fannie Lou Hammer, a Mississippi sharecropper, shouted from her soul: "I'm sick and tired of being sick and tired." She led the first voter-registration drive and in the process was beaten almost to death by the police. Because she had a vision for her people, she continued her fight. She became the founder of the Mississippi Freedom Democratic party. Through her efforts, Black people of Mississippi won the right to vote.

Sometimes it takes a traumatic event to convince people to accept what God is saying. In Noah's day it was the flood. In the days of Jeremiah, it was a devastating war. Jeremiah closed out the book of Lamentations—which means tears—believing that all of his work was in vain and that God had completely forsaken him (see Lamentations 5:20-22).

As hopeless as things might have seemed for Jeremiah, years later the vision continued to speak. A young man named Daniel, a captive in Babylon, discovered a clear vision of God's plan for Israel through the letters of Jeremiah. "I, Daniel, understood…by the word of the LORD given through Jeremiah the prophet, that He would accomplish seventy years in the desolations of Jerusalem" (Daniel 9:2).

The topaz woman holds fast to the vision that the Lord has revealed to her. People might call her an extremist or an eccentric because she doesn't see things as the rest of us do. But if you are a topaz woman of vision, then stand up for what the Lord has revealed in your spirit. It may not be easy, but in the end you will be fully rewarded.

The light of the campfire against Zipporah's dark skin gave her the glow of a fiery, bronze topaz. As the stringed instruments played and the women joined hands and danced in a joyful circle, Zipporah (whose name means "little songbird") lifted her clear soprano voice and sang like an angel.

When she finished singing, everyone was weeping and laughing at the same time. Zipporah trembled with joy as, one by one, the women hugged her neck to let her know they were finally accepting her as one of their own.

"Forgive me for the way I treated you," one old lady cried. Zipporah nodded her head and gave her new friend a second hug.

"Cushite women were born to sing!" a young girl exclaimed to Miriam the sister of Moses, and then she rushed off to embrace Zipporah.

Anger engulfed Miriam as she watched the women gather around her sister-in-law. Miriam was the one who always led the worship songs. *How dare this woman of Ethiopian descent sing praises to the God of the Hebrews,* Miriam thought. In Miriam's eyes, Zipporah was the vile and mysteriously evil woman who had bewitched her younger brother Moses. Miriam, the leader of the Hebrew women and prophetess of God, steadfastly refused to accept an Ethiopian woman as part of her family.

Now, as Miriam stood at the door of her tent watching the women embrace Zipporah, her patience was coming to an end. First it was Jethro, Zipporah's father. This uppity Black man, who called himself a visionary, had somehow persuaded Moses to set seventy elders over the people. The new structure quickly diminished the influence of both Miriam and her brother Aaron, the high priest, as leaders of the people.

"I will never bow to a Black woman," Miriam fumed as she burst into Aaron's tent. "Not only did Moses marry that woman, but he listens to her counsel and that of her worthless father! He should have divorced her long ago!" Miriam raged.

When the Lord heard the evil that Miriam spoke against Moses and his wife, he judged Miriam by turning her skin white with leprosy. The desert winds carried Miriam's howling cries as she wept throughout the night.

"Please do not let her be as one dead!" Aaron pleaded with Moses.

Looking up to heaven Moses fell on his knees and prayed. "It was a foolish mistake, Lord! Please heal her, O God, I pray!"

For seven days Miriam remained in isolation outside the camp. When her leprosy was completely healed, she returned to her people in shame and embarrassment. The spirit of pride that once ruled Miriam's life was completely broken. Now her only desire was to make things right with the people she had wounded.

Zipporah was busy weaving fabric when she looked up and saw Miriam standing in the door of her tent. "Will you forgive me?" Miriam asked trembling with fear.

Zipporah looked at Miriam with loving eyes. "Of course I will. You are my sister, and I pray that you will also be my friend." She smiled and stretched out her arms.

As Miriam and Zipporah wept and embraced, they did not hear Moses enter the tent. His heart rejoiced at the sight of the two women. Now their family was truly one blood and one faith.

Zipporah, whose story here is drawn from Numbers 12, endured years living with in-laws who rejected her because she shared the vision that Moses had for his people. Moses must have come to her after he had seen the burning bush. She was lying next to him when the Lord spoke to him in dreams and visions. She made mistakes along the way, but she was Moses' counselor, encourager, and helpmate from God. As man and wife, they were one flesh. This Black woman also played a key role in freeing the children of Israel.

The book of Job speaks of the price of wisdom as surpassing that of the Ethiopian topaz (see Job 28:18-19). What a fitting way to think of Zipporah, the Ethiopian jewel, who like a shining topaz possessed vision that led to a great reward.

She was a different color and came from a different culture, but Zipporah was blessed to find acceptance in the eyes of Moses, the man she loved. Love and acceptance from one caring person can make you feel confident and beautiful even in the face of rejection from others.

Some years ago the Lord gave me a clear vision that it was time to leave my home in Los Angeles to accept a job with a major media company in the small town of Virginia Beach, Virginia. I felt good about the move, especially since I wanted to get my twelve-year-old daughter away from the hustle and bustle of Los Angeles. I arrived at my new job with braided hair and a colorful dress accessorized with African jewelry. I felt cold stares as I was escorted to my new office. If you're an African-American woman working in White corporate America, you know the story.

In the past my daughter's classmates had been a wide variety of races and nationalities, but the top prep school in our new community had never had a Black student. Together we had to decide whether she was up to the challenge of attending a school whose students and teachers were all White Southerners.

Like Zipporah, we had a clear vision of where God was leading us. So I took on the new job, and my daughter took on the new school. Each morning we would pray together and recite our Scripture. Every morning our ritual was the same. We looked at each other and said: "Remember, people don't have to like us, but they do have to respect us!"

My daughter and I faced many challenges during our first year in southern Virginia, but God's love and the love that we had for each other strengthened and sustained us. The ultimate gift from God was finding a warm and loving African-American church family that overflowed with hospitality. I will always give thanks to God for the friendship of Bishop Rudolph Lewis, his wife Maureen, and their children. Black people in the South have such a strong sense of family. They know how to build confidence and make others feel beautiful and accepted whether they're related or not. The Lewis clan welcomed my daughter and me into the fold and loved all of our hurts away.

Women of African descent have learned to survive as outsiders by drawing strength from family and friends who share a common culture and heritage. We also find love and acceptance from those of other races who appreciate us as human beings. Most important, we've learned to look beyond the boundaries of discrimination to see God's vision for our lives.

Vision, by definition, is a message from the Lord that comes to us while we are awake. It may be a warning or a disclosure about things to come. It may also include instructions about what the Lord wants us to do. When the vision comes alive in your mind, it is not yet reality. Bringing a vision to reality takes faith, patience, and courage. Sometimes people will support and encourage you; other times you will travel with only one unseen companion, the precious Holy Spirit. You will travel through valleys of fear, mountains of obstacles, deserts of trial and error, and rivers of rejection, but the more difficult the journey, the greater the reward.

I celebrate Black Christian women who have stood alone in places dominated by men or people of other races or faiths. While few may recognize our courage and the sacrifices we've made, people do see the release of beauty and power as the Lord brings to pass the vision for our lives.

I believe the Lord gives us these visions for several reasons.

1. To encourage us and stir our faith. "After these things the word of the LORD came to Abram in a vision, saying, 'Do not be afraid, Abram. I am your shield, your exceedingly great reward' " (Genesis 15:1). When the Lord first spoke to Abram in a vision, it was hard for him to believe what God was saying. Abram responded to the Lord as would anyone who could see only the present and not the future. He and his wife were old and had no children, yet the Lord said his reward would be great. He assured him that his descendants would be more than the stars that filled the sky (see verse 5). The vision was enough to persuade Abram that even though he had not yet received what his heart desired, it would eventually come to pass. In the same manner, the woman who hears from God finds peace and renewed faith in the things that God has promised, even though they cannot yet been seen.

2. To stretch us beyond our human understanding. "I looked into it and saw four-footed animals of the earth, wild beasts, reptiles, and birds of the air. Then I heard a voice telling me, 'Get up, Peter. Kill and eat' " (Acts 11:6-7, NIV). Peter saw a sheet in his vision that held a collection of unclean animals that the Lord instructed him to eat. Peter, being a devout Jew, refused to eat anything that was unclean, but the Lord rebuked Peter: "Do not call anything impure that God has made clean" (verse 9, NIV).

Peter's vision from the Lord was to prepare him to minister to a group of Gentiles. The Lord broke down the walls of discrimination within Peter's own heart and used him to minister faith in Jesus Christ to Gentiles. In the same manner, the Lord knows that there are areas in our lives where we are blinded by our own ignorance. The Lord often uses a vision to stretch our understanding and show us the rewards that come with submitting to his will.

3. To give us a clear direction for our lives. "And a vision appeared to Paul in the night. A man of Macedonia stood and pleaded with him, saying, 'Come over to Macedonia and help us'" (Acts 16:9). As the apostle Paul went out to preach the gospel, at times the Holy Spirit would change his course and not allow him to go into certain cities. On one particular journey Paul saw a vision of a man begging him to come and help his people. Many times we are moving in a particular direction when suddenly our progress is blocked. When this happens many people become frustrated and blame their hindrances on the Enemy. But it is not unusual for the topaz woman to be guided by a vision from the Lord that takes her in a completely new direction. She must trust that the Lord is ordering her footsteps.

It was cold and dark, and the rain was falling in buckets as Kiy struggled to run across the muddy field. There was no turning back. If she wanted to survive, she would have to reach the high wall and find a way to climb over.

"This is not how it was supposed to be," she sobbed as she slipped and fell into a deep puddle of mud. She wanted to die on that spot, to never get up again, but someone was yelling her name. "Kiy! Get up! We're almost there... Don't give up, Kiy!" As the lightning flashed across the sky, Kiy caught a glimpse of Betty. Her friend was standing just a few feet away, covered with mud and trying to catch her breath.

"Kiy, you've got to get up. Now!" Betty made her way over to where her friend had fallen and helped her to her feet.

"This is not the way it's supposed to be!" Kiy sobbed.

"But it's the way it is!" Betty shouted. "Let's go. We're almost there."

The wall seemed to tower to the sky as the two girls approached the final leg of their journey. With another flash of lightning, they spotted a knotted rope that would allow them to climb over it.

"I can't make it... I can't," Kiy whispered.

Betty had no more words of encouragement. She stood in front of the wall, hoping a hand would appear and magically lift them over.

"Get out of the way, stupid losers!" A White man twice their size slammed them into the wall and grabbed the rope.

A burning rage engulfed Kiy and Betty. They could no longer feel the rain and cold, only the flood of anger that suddenly energized them.

Kiy let out a primal scream she as watched the bulky shadow of the man climbing up the rope. "Losers? Just wait till we get our hands on you!"

By the time Kiy and Betty climbed over the high wall, the man was gone, but their sergeant was waiting. "Well, looks like you girls are going to make your graduation after all," he said with indifference.

A week later the president of the United States stood at the podium of the West Point Military Academy to address the graduates. Kiy and Betty sat on the platform in their spotless white uniforms, looking out at the stadium of friends and family members who had come for the ceremony.

"Wow! My vision has finally come true. This is how I dreamed it was going to be," Kiy whispered to Betty.

When the president called Kiy's name, she walked across the stage and received her degree. Heading back to her seat with Betty close behind, she stopped for a moment and took one last look at the cadets sitting on the platform.

"What are you looking at?" Betty whispered. "You're holding up the line!"

"I'm looking for that guy who called me a loser. I want to take him to lunch before I leave West Point."*

Thus says the LORD:
"Refrain your voice from weeping,
And your eyes from tears;
For your work shall be rewarded."

JEREMIAH 31:16

---

* In June 2002, I traveled to New York to attend the graduation of Kiyneischa Lover and Betty Coles from West Point Military Academy. I continue to pray for them as they, at the time of this writing, are stationed together in South Korea.

Chapter 7

The Beauty of Aquamarine

A Woman Who Dwells in Peace

He leads me beside quiet waters,

he restores my soul.

PSALM 23:2-3, NIV

Aquamarine appears as the third jewel on Aaron's breastplate, but a bit of clarification is needed regarding this jewel. Depending upon the translation you are reading, the third jewel might be called beryl, aquamarine, or emerald. This is because aquamarines and emeralds are both in the beryl family. The emerald is the green version of beryl, and the aquamarine is the blue-green version. As I stated earlier, a great deal of uncertainty surrounds the accurate names of the jewels on Aaron's breastplate. But the oldest Hebrew translation identifies the third jewel in Aaron's breastplate as beryl.

The jewel was inscribed with the name of Zebulun, the sixth son of Leah and Jacob. The name Zebulun means "to dwell." In Genesis 49:13, Jacob prophesied that Zebulun would dwell by the seashore and become the haven for ships. Many scholars believe that the descendants of Zebulun lived near the sea and thrived as merchants (see Deuteronomy 33:18-19).

For this reason I suspect the jewel was aquamarine beryl, for the name aquamarine means "seawater."

In the biblical context, the light blue color of aquamarine symbolizes peace and the presence of God. Light blue is also connected to the life-giving properties of water, where thirst is satisfied, plants and trees are nourished, and all of creation is cleansed and refreshed. Water also represents peace and tranquility for those who dwell beside "quiet waters."

The aquamarine jewel is a reminder that when a woman of African ancestry becomes a peaceful dwelling, she sparkles with the beauty of calm, blue waters. Her words are as restful as the sound of a rippling brook. She brings a sense of calm to those who are caught in the storms of life. Like a beacon of hope shining in the darkness, she guides those who are troubled to the true Source of all peace: the Lord Jesus Christ.

A man who shares his life with a peaceful woman is blessed indeed. Being with her is like coming home to a quiet house after spending a long, stressful day in the rat race. The woman who is as comforting as an aquamarine jewel is not passive, but she knows how to pick her battles. She's like a skilled ambassador; when challenges arise she presents her case or negotiates her position with precision timing. She makes sure that her man is not hungry or tired when it is necessary to deal with tough issues. Her soft words find their way into his heart without disturbing his peace. She is gifted at dealing with sensitive matters without starting a war in her household. Whatever life brings, her priority and her goal are to live in peace.

Peace should never be mistaken for calm. Calm is a pleasant atmosphere with a restful environment. Peace is completely different. Peace means to experience an atmosphere of rest even in the midst of a storm.

I recently learned about this firsthand when I found myself dealing with an unusual amount of stress. My father had become seriously ill, which added an even greater burden to my overloaded schedule. And to top things off, my daughter asked me to take care of her two dogs, Peace and Joy, because she had to make a weekend ministry trip. So I found myself taking care of a sick father, two dogs, *and* my five-year-old nephew, Manny, whose mother was under the weather. I had a stack of work to complete, and a writing deadline loomed over me. Needless to say, peace was nowhere to be found. By the time my daughter returned from her trip and my nephew went back to his mother, I felt as if I had run a marathon.

Whenever I'm under a lot of pressure, it has been my practice to walk in the mountains near my house. The sight of trees and rolling hillsides always revives my spirit. On the dirt trails that lead into the mountains, I can talk to the Lord without being interrupted and then quietly listen while he speaks to my soul.

After my hectic weekend, I really needed to be refreshed. I was like a child heading for the playground as I parked my car at the foot of the trail and got my walking stick out of the trunk. Just as I started up the dirt road, I heard a car horn honking. I turned around to see my daughter and Manny waving at me, with her two dogs in tow.

"Wow, this is great! I can't believe we ran into each other," Theresa smiled and gave me a big hug. "I thought Manny and I would take Peace and Joy for a walk before he goes to school." She was chattering away as the parade of dogs and the five-year-old followed me up the trail.

Moments later Manny was whining because he fell down trying to hold onto Joy's leash. Next, my daughter had to chase away a strange dog that came out of nowhere, barking at Peace. I felt as if I were climbing the mountain trail with a load of bricks on my back. I wasn't listening to Theresa, but right in the middle of her spiel, she looked at her watch and realized she had to rush to drop Manny off at school.

"Mom, could you keep an eye on the dogs while I take Manny to school? I'll be back in ten minutes."

She and Manny retreated down the trail. As soon as she was out of sight, Peace and Joy yanked themselves free from their leashes and headed straight up the hill in the direction of a cliff that drops off into a deep canyon. I panicked and chased them up the trail screaming, "Peace! Joy! Come back here, now! Peace! Joy! Where are you?" I spotted a shortcut through a lush green meadow that led to the top of the hill. As I ran quickly through the grass, I didn't notice the beautiful maze of sprawling oak trees, nor did I look up above at the billowing clouds in the crystal blue sky. I ran as fast as I could, shouting at the top of my lungs: "Peace! Joy! Where are you? Peace! Joy! Come back! Peace! Joy! Peace…please come back! Joy, where are you?"

As I continued to cry out for Peace and Joy, the overwhelming presence of God engulfed me. I was still shouting, but now the words had new meaning: "Peace, where are you? I need peace! Please, Lord. Give me back my peace. Lord, I need joy. Lord, give me back my joy…please, Lord."

My face wet with tears, I sat down in the middle of that green meadow and looked up to heaven, worshiping and praising the Lord. "You make me lie down in green pastures," I whispered. Time seemed to stand still until the silence was interrupted by the faint sound of panting dogs. When I opened my eyes, Peace was sitting quietly next to me. Moments later, Joy was running across the meadow wagging her tail. She came to me and licked my hand.

At that moment this scripture came to mind: "You will keep him in perfect peace, whose mind is stayed on You, because he trusts in You" (Isaiah 26:3). I learned on that day that when you seek the Lord, you will soon find peace and joy.

The woman who possesses the spirit of peace may not dwell in a restful environment (few of us do!), but the chaos is exactly what causes the peace within her soul to shine like a beautiful aquamarine jewel. Not only does she have the gift of personal peace, but she also possesses the spirit of a peacemaker. Matthew 5:9 tells us, "Blessed are the peacemakers, for they shall be called [daughters] of God."

The peacemaker is a woman of prayer and godliness. People respect her ability to help others resolve their differences. She demonstrates self-control and quiet composure in the most stressful situations. She places the value of peace far above her personal desires and will do all in her power to keep the peace.

In stark contrast, a woman without peace dwells in a place where she is unfulfilled, troubled, and dissatisfied. In this unhappy dwelling place, the attributes that make a woman feel beautiful have been stripped away. This woman often loses her desire to dress up, fix her hair, and look pretty, because outer beauty is a reflection of inward contentment. Even if she is dressed up and beautiful to look at, her attractiveness flees like a bird once she begins to trouble the waters. The man in her life either lives in torment or will give up and head for the hills. Listen to what the Bible says about a woman who is not peaceful: "Better to live in a desert than with a quarrelsome and ill-tempered [woman]" (Proverbs 21:19, NIV).

If you are a balanced and loving woman of color, you want peace in your dwelling place. In your quest to find the spirit of peace, I pray that you would come to understand that the precious jewel of peace is sometimes found in the most unlikely places. I have been in the homes of wealthy people who possessed everything money could buy, yet they had no peace of mind. On the other hand, I have walked into hospital rooms where, in spite of pain and sickness, I could sense the presence of God's peace. And I have talked to women in prison cells who seemed to have more peace than people who are free. I have learned that peace will dwell wherever it is welcomed and cherished.

Laylah walked along the shallow edge of the Mediterranean Sea, gathering tiny shellfish that looked like worthless pebbles washed ashore by the morning tide. But the shellfish that filled Laylah's shoulder sack contained a rare purple dye that would be sold to wealthy Greek, Roman, and Egyptian merchants.

With her skirt pulled up and the hem tucked into her waist, Laylah stood in the water, shouting commands at the women and children who worked for her father: "Work faster! If you don't hurry, others will come and rob us of our harvest!" The cuts in Laylah's fingers and feet from gathering shellfish and the dull ache in her back were made bearable by thoughts of a new set of silver bracelets and the fine fabric she would receive in exchange for the costly purple dye.

As a young woman working with her father, Laylah had learned foreign languages that allowed her to negotiate with the merchants from distant lands. She took pride in using her innocent eyes and soft voice to outsmart her customers. Laylah became skilled in making a good profit by bartering down to the wire for her desired price.

"Someday I will be a wealthy woman," she said to her father later that day as they looked over their harvest.

His answer was always the same whenever they talked about her future. "Money isn't everything. Life, love, and peace of mind are the true gifts from God."

His words meant little to Laylah. She had visions of living in a fine house, being surrounded by servants, and traveling to far-off lands. No longer would her hands be cut and stained with purple dye; they would be covered with precious jewels.

The next day Laylah's heart was heavy as she watched her father's servants packing the vats of purple dye that would be loaded onto the waiting ships.

"But why can't I go with you?" she pleaded with her father. "Why do I have to hear from the workers about the great cities of Athens, Crete, Cyprus, and the beauty of Egypt? Please! Take me with you, Father, just this one time," Laylah pleaded.

"You already know my answer." Her father tried to ignore his willful daughter. "A merchant ship is no place for a young woman."

"But, Father, I work so hard. Please grant me this one request," she begged.

For a long time Laylah's father studied her face, which was the color of strong coffee from working in the hot sun. He looked at her rough hands. She was a jewel who deserved more than he could ever give her. "God has given you the gift of persuasion." He smiled at Laylah. "Tomorrow I will break every rule, and you will board the ship."

Laylah's heart leaped for joy as she hugged her father's neck, and she went away to prepare for her journey.

The next day dawned bright and fair as the merchants boarded the ship and weighed it down with endless containers of purple dye, bolts of purple fabric, cords of timber, barrels of salt crystals, blown glass, and dried fish. When their work was done, they set sail, a warm breeze escorting the ship gently over the rolling waves. The Phoenician shoreline slowly disappeared from view. Laylah's heart beat with excitement as she listened to the merchants tell stories, wrestle with one another on the deck of the ship, and sing joyful songs.

The following morning she awoke from her sleep anticipating another day of sunny skies and wonderful storytelling. But to her surprise the sky was dark and ominous, and the sailors hurried about the ship tying down cargo and securing the sails.

"I'm afraid we're heading into a storm, and there's no way to avoid it." Laylah's father tried to sound lighthearted as he led his daughter to a lower part of the ship where they would ride out the tempest. Fear gripped Laylah's heart as the sky clapped its hands with a thunderous noise and the ship pitched and rolled, tossing anything that was not securely fastened. As the angry rain and waves beat against the ship, every available man worked feverishly, bailing water and dumping timber, salt, fabric, and dye overboard to keep the ship from sinking. Laylah lay huddled in a corner praying. "Lord, please don't take away all that we've worked for."

As soon as the words left her mouth, a fierce wind lifted the ship to the heavens and then slammed it down into the depths of the sea. Laylah gasped for air as the water poured in through every opening. At that moment God was speaking, but Laylah did not understand the words written on the stormy wind: "When your merchandise went out on the seas, you satisfied many nations; with your great wealth and your wares you enriched the kings of the earth. Now you are shattered by the sea in the depths of the waters; your wares and all your company have gone down with you" (Ezekiel 27:33-34, NIV).

"Father!" Laylah screamed as she held on to whatever she could find. Horrible thoughts invaded her mind. What if her father had been washed overboard? What if she had lost him forever? How could she live without him?

"Lord, where are you?" Laylah cried out. "Forgive me, Lord…have mercy! I don't care about riches…just let me see my father again." As the ship continued to rock and reel on the stormy sea, a feeling of calm washed over Laylah, calm such as she had never known before. It was as if God's unseen arms were protecting her from the raging storm. Now she could hear a voice swirling in the wind. "Peace, be still."

Soon the heavy rain slowed to a light trickle, and the darkness in the sky rolled back like an ebony curtain. Laylah made her way to the top deck where the men were trying to salvage what the storm had not washed away.

"Father! Where are you?" Laylah cried out.

"I'm here Laylah… I'm here," he answered. When she found him, his forehead was covered with blood.

"Are you all right?" Laylah cried as she ran to his side and touched his head.

"I'm fine, Daughter. It's just a scratch where a falling beam hit me during the storm," he tried to reassure her.

On the following day the tattered ship pulled into port with nothing on board except the lives of the sailors and merchants—and one grateful young woman.

"No silver bracelets on this trip." Laylah's father gave her a sad smile.

Laylah hugged him as they watched the sun rise in the morning sky.

"Silver bracelets could never take the place of what I already have. I have my family, I have my life, and I have peace in my heart."

All too often people think that in order to have peace you must have calm surroundings. But real peace is not based on circumstances; it is the Prince of Peace dwelling within us that gives us a sense of peace when storms rage around us.

Those who go down to the sea in ships,
Who do business on great waters,
They see the works of the LORD,
And His wonders in the deep.
For He commands and raises the stormy wind,
Which lifts up the waves of the sea.…
Then they cry out to the LORD in their trouble.…
He calms the storm.…
He guides them to their desired haven. (Psalm 107:23-30)

As women of African heritage, we face many challenges designed to rob us of our peace. Maintaining our peace has a great deal to do with focus. If you were looking at your life through a camera lens, you could choose a narrow focus that would allow you to see only the things that are troubling you. Or you could set your focus on a wide shot and include the opportunities that are birthed out of trouble. In the midst of trouble, focus on these unseen opportunities:

- moving to a new level of faith
- seeing the true commitment of people in your life
- changing your destiny and flow into God's perfect plan
- becoming sensitized to the sufferings of others
- reaching within yourself for the strength, creativity, and resources you never recognized before
- discovering and developing resources that can benefit others
- seeing God move in miraculous ways as you've never before experienced

These are just a few of the blessed opportunities that are disguised as trouble.

Recently, I had a frightening experience concerning my daughter's health. The preliminary diagnosis gave us much cause for alarm, even appearing to be life threatening. I gathered with prayer warriors, and we fell on our knees and cried out to God until the spirit of peace rose up and slew every fearful thought. The battle raged, but soon the spirit of peace completely prevailed.

After days of prayer and fasting, the doctors determined that while my daughter's condition was serious, it was not life threatening. A new level of peace and thanksgiving engulfed our family. When the lens was focused on my daughter's life or death, it was almost too much to bear. But when the picture zoomed out, I could see that the peace of God had been in the picture all along, waiting to show me all the options and possibilities that I had never considered before.

When we encounter difficult circumstances like this, we must remember that God has promised every believer that his peace will always be there to guard us from the attacks of Satan. Picture in your mind Jesus, the Prince of Peace, standing guard over everything that pertains to your life. His appearance is like polished bronze, strong and beautiful. In his left hand is the Word of God and in his right hand a silver sword. The sword has a beautifully carved handle with a swirling pattern of silver and gold set with crystal blue aquamarine jewels. The sword protects you from every demonic host that comes against your health, prosperity, and contentment.

The Word of God is also a weapon against the demonic host. It must be observed at all times if you are to maintain God's peace, God's presence, and God's protection. The following scriptures can serve as ammunition to guard your heart and mind:

"Seek peace and pursue it" (Psalm 34:14). The word *pursue* means "to chase after peace." Determine where peace hangs out. Search for peace in worship services and Bible studies. Seek peace among friends who are sober and mature. Once you capture peace, prepare a place in your heart where it can continuously dwell. Remember, once the spirit of peace comes to dwell with you, you must guard your heart and mind. Don't be a drama queen. Place a sign on the door of your heart that says: No More Drama.

"He will keep in perfect peace all those who trust in him, whose thoughts turn often to the Lord!" (Isaiah 26:3, TLB). Thoughts can be like a storage pantry where you keep a fresh supply of godly teachings and beliefs that nourish you with peace. If the pantry is filled with a lot of negative thoughts and old ideas, there's no room on the shelves for a fresh supply of godly teachings. Perhaps it's time to clean house. If you want to have perfect peace, begin with a perfect storage pantry of godly thoughts and beliefs. Throw out unforgiveness and dump past hurts into the trash. Sweep away toxic people and maybe even a toxic job situation. Get rid of all of the fantasies and replace them with the reality of God's Word.

"Great peace have those who love Your law, and nothing causes them to stumble" (Psalm 119:165). Because I go hiking on a regular basis, I make sure to wear a good pair of hiking shoes and carry a sturdy walking stick that will keep me from stumbling on the steep mountain trails. Similarly, to maintain your peace as you travel the rough terrain of this world, the laws of God serve to help you balance your life and keep you from stumbling. Obedience to the law of God will keep you from making foolish decisions that cause you to stumble into sin. Most sins are not premeditated. A teenage girl didn't intend to get pregnant. She just ended up in a situation where things went too far. The law of God helps us set boundaries that are designed not to restrict us from enjoying life, but to help us keep our balance and avoid the kinds of trouble that rob us of our peace. When we walk in God's law, he promises that we will have a life filled with peace. "The ways of the LORD are right; the righteous walk in them, but the rebellious stumble in them" (Hosea 14:9, NIV).

David glared into the mirror, not really looking at his own reflection. Instead he was reflecting on the stupid problems that were sending his marriage into a tailspin. Amani, his wife of twelve years, was acting like a spoiled child, complaining about the most ridiculous things: a few girlie magazines and some harmless fun on the Internet. Why was she trippin' so hard? It wasn't like he was having an affair. *Maybe she's feeling insecure because of her sudden weight gain,* he thought.

David shook his head as he remembered the terrible scene the night before when Amani stormed downstairs and confronted him because he was looking at nude women on the Internet. "If you're so crazy about big boobs and blonde hair, why did you marry me? I guess I'm not good enough for you anymore!" She had yelled so loud that the kids woke up and came into the hallway to see what was wrong. *What was her problem?* David wondered.

In the kitchen, Amani was stirring a pot of grits and wiping the tears from her eyes. She wasn't crying about what had happened with David the night before. She was remembering how her father preferred her younger sister because she had soft hazel eyes and curly hair. Amani looked more like her mother's side of the family—woolly hair and a thick frame. She had always been a pretty girl herself, with smooth olive skin, but not her sister's type of pretty, the kind that made her father's eyes light up.

Now it was the same thing all over again with David: nude women with slender bodies and silky hair. *How could he be so heartless? How could he call himself a Christian and act like a degenerate?* Amani turned off the burner. Her heaviness was so great that she sat down at the kitchen table to think and to pray. "Lord, I don't know where to turn," she whispered. "It's like Satan is trying to take control of my family...and I feel like I'm fighting a losing battle. Lord, please help me." Amani wiped the tears away and opened the Bible. She read: "Be anxious for nothing, but in everything by prayer and supplication, with thanksgiving, let your requests be made known to God; and the peace of God, which surpasses all understanding, will guard your hearts and minds through Christ Jesus" (Philippians 4:6-7).

Back in the bedroom, David straightened his necktie and slipped on his jacket. *Maybe a trial separation is what we need,* David thought. *Then Amani might start showing me some respect for all my hard work.* His mind made up, David headed downstairs to tell Amani what he'd decided. As he reached the foot of the stairs and walked into the living room, a strange feeling engulfed him. From the kitchen he could hear his wife's voice. She was talking to someone in a tone so gentle and loving that he stopped in the middle of the room to listen. "I love him so… Please, Lord, give us back the love and peace that we once shared."

David's eyes grew moist as he listened to his wife's tender words. He moved to the kitchen doorway and watched as she sat at the table with her hands lifted in praise. For some reason she wasn't startled when he walked up behind her and touched her shoulders. "I'm sorry I hurt you. I'm sorry about the fantasies. I must be crazy to be spending time checking out the Internet when I already have the real thing."

Let the peace of Christ rule in your hearts,
since as members of one body you
were called to peace. And be thankful.

Colossians 3:15, NIV

Chapter 8

The Beauty of Turquoise

A Woman of Mercy and Grace

O afflicted city, lashed by storms and not comforted,
I will build you with stones of turquoise,
your foundations with sapphires.

ISAIAH 54:11, NIV

According to the original Hebrew writings, the turquoise stone was the fourth jewel mounted on Aaron's breastplate. The name engraved on it was Reuben, the eldest of the twelve sons of Jacob. A close translation of his name would be "see, or behold, a son." Overcome with the sorrow of being unloved by her husband, Leah stretched the meaning of her son's name from "see a son" to "God sees my affliction" (see Genesis 29:32).

Turquoise is as different from its three predecessors—ruby, topaz, and aquamarine—as African women with bronze skin and woolly hair are different from European women with silky hair. The first three jewels on the breastplate are strong, transparent, and reflect light. Turquoise, however, is a soft stone with a smooth blue-green surface that is easily cracked or broken. Because it is not clear and transparent, its beauty is not due to its ability to sparkle and reflect light. Natural light cannot penetrate turquoise. Instead, it possesses a unique luminous glow.

Egyptians, among others, mined the precious jewel as far back as 3000 B.C. Its smooth, bold blue-green color added richness to the crowns of kings and queens and beauty to their most cherished works of art. This was especially true when the turquoise jewel was laced with natural thin streaks of copper and other colorful minerals.

Reuben's personality seems perfectly suited to the fragile blue-green stone that bears his name. Reuben's merciful heart was clearly seen when he was used by God to save his brother Joseph from being murdered by members of his own family (see Genesis 37:20-21). This contrasts with his dark mistake that cost him the position and privileges of the firstborn son: Reuben engaged in an intimate relationship with his father's concubine Bilhah (see Genesis 35:22). Consequently, scholars believe, Reuben's name is not listed first on Aaron's breastplate (the position of the eldest son); instead, his name is listed fourth.

The story of Reuben's sin offers more than a lesson about the consequences of moral failure; it reveals God's desire to redeem our sin and use our brokenness to help others. No one can understand another person's need for mercy and grace like one who has made a major mistake that, by human standards, can never be erased. Though Reuben may have shared his brothers' frustration with Joseph's seemingly arrogant behavior, because of his own past sin, Reuben understood Joseph's need for grace and mercy. He talked his clan of jealous brothers out of killing Joseph, their father's favorite son (see Genesis 37:18-29).

Like Reuben's, your imperfect life can be used by God. No matter how badly you've blown it, he sees beyond your faults. God sees the value of your dark experience, and God sees how he will transform your life and use you to his glory in the days to come. You may have been involved in drugs, prostitution, or fraud, or had multiple abortions. But know that from the beginning to the end, God sees—and he has a beautiful plan for your life.

The trouble with sin is that it blinds us to the depths of God's mercy and grace, preventing us from embracing his forgiveness. I used to suffer from tremendous guilt; it triggered anxiety attacks and depression. To numb my shame and remorse, I took tranquilizers, cocaine, and alcohol and tried a long list of forgotten men; nothing succeeded in making me happy.

One Christmas I sent my two daughters to Philadelphia to spend the holidays with my parents. When I put my daughters on the plane, I promised to follow in a few days. It was the time of year I hated the most. After losing my husband to cancer and going through a major financial struggle, I wasn't big on holidays and celebrations. The few days turned into a week of drinking and snorting cocaine in a high-rise condo in Holly-wood. The party was nonstop—food, liquor, and good music flowed freely as I mingled with an intimate group of beautiful and talented people.

My new boyfriend was a drug dealer, which meant that I could have all the drugs I wanted, free. His wares kept me from thinking, feeling, or dealing with my life. Like so many Black women with no husband and young children, I was looking, in my own twisted way, for a man to offer financial security, even though the money was illegal. I sat up night after night drinking, doing drugs, and participating in all the things that come with that lifestyle. Finally, on Christmas Eve I pulled myself together, packed a suitcase, and headed for Philadelphia. The day after Christmas my boyfriend/supplier was arrested in a drug bust. Eventually, he was sent to prison for a long time. When I heard the news of the bust, I was numb with the realization that instead of being with my children, I could have been in jail.

Long before the Lord transformed my life, his mercy and grace were already at work on my behalf. When the light of truth exposed my foolish mistakes, I learned the power of God's mercy. Despite all the drugs I had experimented with, I never became addicted and was never arrested. It wasn't because I had such a strong will, but because the Lord supernaturally protected me from the traps of Satan.

Mercy is the gift of God that covers our sins and protects us from the penalties of God's law. Mercy is the Lord blessing us with what we don't deserve, while keeping us from the punishment we do deserve. Grace is another word for God's goodness. It gives us the divine ability to break free from the bondage of sin, which we could never accomplish in our own strength. Looking back, I can clearly see that goodness and mercy have followed me all the days of my life (see Psalm 23:6).

The luminous glow of the turquoise symbolizes the forgiven woman who possesses the beauty of humility. She knows from personal experience that nothing but God's grace brought her out of all of her dark experiences. To everyone's surprise, she is becoming a blessing in the lives of the same people who once cursed her name.

Developing the gift of mercy and grace should come easily for women of color, because in a time when we could have been completely destroyed as a people, God's mercy and grace kept us alive. Women with the greatest gift of mercy and grace are those who once lived against the dark backdrop of suffering or the practice of sin with all its terrible consequences.

Often when our lives become a real mess, we think there is no hope for change. Or we can look at others who have done a terrible wrong and think they will never change. But the Lord is a recycler. Sometimes he allows people to hit rock bottom and even stay there for a while. Then, and only then, his deliverance will come and he will use them for his glory. The Lord will sometimes let everything fall apart in our lives so that when restoration comes, we will not be prideful. We will know without a doubt that nothing but the mercy and grace of God saved us from destruction.

God delights in using the most unlikely people to do the most effective ministry. Jesus restored Peter even though he denied him three times, and Jesus made Peter his "rock," the leader of the church. The same grace that God showed to Peter is the grace that allows us to find permanent deliverance from alcohol, drugs, and even toxic relationships. Grace is God's strength that can be clearly seen in our weakness (see 2 Corinthians 12:9).

The woman's heart is beating as fast as raindrops falling in a summer storm. She looks anxiously into the mirror, wipes away the last of the makeup from her face, and pulls her hair back with a plain scarf. Before leaving her house, she picks up a small, beautifully carved alabaster box and carefully places it in the sack that hangs on her shoulder. With one deep breath the woman gathers her courage and steps into the street.

"Where are you going?" a neighbor yells from a nearby window.

"To see a man!" the woman replies as she hurries along.

"Of course! But where are your fancy clothes?" the neighbor teases.

The woman carrying the alabaster box does not reply. She is too busy wondering if she will arrive on time. Worried that she might miss her one chance to see Jesus face to face, she quickens her hurried steps into a trot, and then she is breathlessly running though the streets with tears streaming down her face.

"Wait for me…please wait," she whispers as the house where Jesus is dining comes into view.

The servants standing in the courtyard are big and strong enough to restrain the panting woman from entering the house, but the shock of her hurried words and her unbroken stride freezes them in their tracks and they allow her to pass.

"I have a gift for Jesus. I must see him! I must give him his gift," she explains as she enters Simon's, where Jesus is having dinner with a group of religious leaders.

The woman has never seen Jesus face to face, but she knows him by the compassion in his eyes and his merciful smile. She is weak and trembling all over as she falls to her knees. For what seems a lifetime, she is bent over weeping and kissing Jesus' feet. She is weeping with sorrow for all of her foolish sins, but she is also weeping with joy because she knows she is alive only by the mercy of God. Now she has a chance to change and serve God for the rest of her days.

The fountain of tears falling from the woman's eyes washes the dust from the feet of Jesus. She unties her scarf and uses her hair to wipe the tears from his feet. In silent embarrassment, everyone present witnesses her brazen display. The woman is unaware of the mounting tension as she removes the alabaster box from her shoulder pouch. With one swift blow, she breaks open the container, and the room is filled with a sweet fragrance that overwhelms the senses. She hears Jesus speaking to Simon and the others:

"Her sins, which are many, are forgiven, for she loved much" (Luke 7:47). The words have no meaning to the woman because she is caught up in a personal symphony of praise. Then, Jesus touches her shoulder and says, "Your sins are forgiven.... Your faith has saved you. Go in peace" (verses 48-50).

She leaves the house feeling clean and purified. She had been washed in the river of mercy and grace, and now God's love covers her with a fragrance far sweeter than any perfume that could be poured from an alabaster box.

This story, retold from Luke 7, reveals the mercy Jesus extended to the woman who washed his feet with her tears. He overlooked her sinful condition and responded to her need to be forgiven. He also extended his grace by forgiving her sins and saving her soul.

The book of Hebrews encourages us to come to the Lord with the same bold expectation as the woman who dared to barge into the house of a religious leader in hopes of finding redemption: "For we do not have a high priest who is unable to sympathize with our weaknesses, but we have one who has been tempted in every way, just as we are—yet was without sin. Let us then approach the throne of grace with confidence, so that we may receive mercy and find grace to help us in our time of need" (4:15-16, NIV).

The apostle Paul knew firsthand the power of God's mercy and grace. He referred to himself as the chief sinner (see 1 Timothy 1:15), because before his conversion he killed Christians and sent them to prison. But after his miraculous encounter with Jesus, he became one of the leaders of the Christian church and a major New Testament writer. With his past life clearly etched in his mind, Paul wrote: "I became a servant of this gospel by the gift of God's grace given me through the working of his power. Although I am less than the least of all God's people, this grace was given me" (Ephesians 3:7-8, NIV).

You may feel unworthy of God's mercy or believe you will spend the rest of your life being punished for your sins. Just as natural light cannot penetrate the turquoise jewel, only the light of God's mercy and grace overrides his penalty of sin in your life. It allows you to overcome the darkest situation. "Mercy triumphs over judgment" (James 2:13)!

Your heavenly Father loves you in spite of your weaknesses and even your sinful behavior. When God is the judge, it is safe to throw yourself on the mercy of the court. "But God, who is rich in mercy, because of His great love with which He loved us" (Ephesians 2:4).

If you want to get your life on the right track, but you're not sure what to do or say, pray this simple prayer:

> Lord, I confess to you that I have sinned, and now I ask that you
> forgive me for the wrong I have done and the people I have hurt.
> I ask you, Jesus, to come into my heart and be my Lord and Savior.
> Wash away my guilt and shame. Make me clean and pure in your
> sight. Speak to my heart and show me what direction to take so I
> can learn how to live a life that is pleasing to you. When I read the
> Bible, give me understanding. Give me a pastor and teachers who
> can help me grow spiritually. I ask all of these things in the name
> of Jesus. Amen.

If you prayed those words—or something similar in the past—here's what you can expect from the mercy and grace of God:

God's mercy will allow you to make mistakes without experiencing the full consequences of your actions. I can remember a time as a young girl when my life became so unbearable that I tried to commit suicide. The doctor said I survived because the pills I took were very old and had lost their potency. But looking back, I know God's mercy saved my life.

God's mercy will allow you to be hurt now so you won't be completely destroyed later. Once my heart was broken when a man I thought I was in love with decided to end our relationship. I pleaded with God to bring him back, but it didn't happen. He married someone else and became an abusive alcoholic.

God's mercy will make a way for you to face an impossible situation. When the doctors thought I had breast cancer, my mother went boldly to the throne of grace to ask for God's mercy. She laid her hands on me and prayed like I never heard her pray before. When I went into surgery to have the tumor removed, no cancer was found in my body.

God's grace will give you the ability to accomplish things you could not do in your own strength. I prayed and asked the Lord to give me more strength and power. I was able to write two books while working, attending seminary, and taking care of my ill father full time. I know that nothing but the supernatural grace of God kept me going.

God's grace will cover your shortcomings. I remember taking a class that was so difficult I thought I would fail. My twenty-page research paper was nowhere near completed by the due date. I worked night and day, but I still didn't finish the project. When I went to my professor to plead for an extension, I learned that I had a wrong date and the paper wasn't due for another week.

God's grace will supply all of your needs when you run out of resources. A few weeks after I started writing my first book, my computer crashed and couldn't be fixed. I had no money to replace it, so I had to put the project on hold. After I spoke at a church a few weeks later, a young woman whom I had never seen before walked up to me and gave me a check for three thousand dollars.

Becoming a woman of mercy and grace is the most fabulous beauty treatment I know. It will make you glow like a turquoise jewel. In the past, women of African ancestry were well known for their gifts of mercy and grace. The merciful Black woman shared her home or raised the children who were left with no one to care for them. If someone had no job or food to eat, the merciful Black woman always helped out until times got better.

The man in a turquoise woman's life is especially blessed. She is especially effective with hard cases. In marriage, she has a special way of ministering to the husband who becomes easily frustrated and then makes a wrong decision. She knows how to pray and help her man find his way back to a right path, because a turquoise woman never loses sight of her own weaknesses and shortcomings. She understands the process of getting right with the Lord.

Because of her joy in God's forgiveness, a turquoise woman often champions the causes of the poor and needy, desiring to share the beauty she's discovered.

The first time I visited a woman's prison, I had all kinds of preconceived notions as to what type of women I would be dealing with. I thought I would be talking with women who lacked education, refinement, and spiritual insight. I thought it was my duty to help raise them to a higher level of dignity and humanity. But walking through the doors of Framingham Penitentiary just outside of Boston, Massachusetts, changed my attitude forever.

On my first of many visits, I was greeted by a beautiful group of mostly Black and Brown women who were filled with love, kindness, and dignity. After the worship service, I met a woman who was affectionately known as Momma Lucy. This full-bodied, honey-colored woman with a big warm smile was serving a life sentence for murdering the husband who had abused her for years. Known for leading prayer and Bible study and encouraging women who wanted to give up on life, Momma Lucy wore mercy and truth like a beautiful turquoise necklace (see Proverbs 3:3). I also met accountants, schoolteachers, and young moms who found themselves involved in situations that ended with their incarceration. Many of these women were once very successful. They never dreamed that the circumstances of their lives would take a drastic turn, leading them to forfeit their families, their children, and their futures.

If you are a woman of African ancestry, the racial injustices of the prison system, the court system, and other institutions are realities. If you are in a situation where you don't have good health insurance or you are forced to seek welfare assistance, you may find that mercy and grace are rare jewels indeed. However, the challenges we face develop the gifts of mercy and compassion in our hearts. The most important lesson we learn when we are in need of mercy and grace is that only a strong relationship with God can protect us from the demons of injustice. Failures and disappointments in life can crown you either with mercy and grace or with anger and bitterness.

Yet those days without trials can be a danger to our inner beauty as well if we allow them to draw our focus off God. When I meet women who are experiencing the overflowing blessings of the Lord, I rejoice with them. I celebrate the scripture that says, "I pray that you may prosper in all things and be in health, just as your soul prospers" (3 John 2). The soul is of more value than the pleasures offered in this world.

As you are blessed with the mercy and grace of God, remember this: Don't allow a proud and haughty spirit to diminish the beautiful gift of mercy and grace that is at work in your life. Do all in your power to demonstrate mercy toward those who are less fortunate than you. Never brag about your success, but give glory to God for his grace. Never make people feel like you're looking down on them or ask why they don't get it together, especially when you don't know the full story. "Pride goes before destruction, and a haughty spirit before a fall" (Proverbs 16:18).

Every time you show mercy and grace to others, you are making an investment in your own future. When you sit up all night taking care of a sick person because you can't stand to see her suffer or go uncared for, God remembers. When you reach into your savings to help someone finish college or to help the ministry without bragging about your good deed, God remembers. When you become a true woman of mercy and grace, you will discover that God will show mercy when you are in need.

Your investment in showing mercy will also cover the people you love. "Blessed are the merciful, for they shall obtain mercy" (Matthew 5:7).

Mercy and grace reveal the true character of God and are a testimony to others of his love for us. Most of us grew up singing "Jesus Loves Me." But it isn't until we personally experience his mercy and grace that we know the true meaning of the song. No one likes feeling completely helpless, but in difficult times we see the tailor-made mercy and grace of God. "I will praise You, O LORD, with my whole heart; I will tell of all Your marvelous works" (Psalm 9:1).

At first the ugly meanness hid behind the pretty faces of the two women who sat in Barry's beauty salon waiting to get their hair done. As usual their target was Rosie, the shop's manager. Rosie's sweet round face was covered with humiliation as Connie, the meaner of the two, began her eloquent harassment while facing the mirror and adjusting the belt around her slim waist.

"If I don't cut back on the sweets, I'm going to start looking like you-know-who." She said the words ever so softly to her friend Sheila.

"Shhh!" Sheila giggled. "She'll hear you."

Connie cut her eyes at Rosie. "Didn't you know? She can't hear good... She's deaf!"

Rosie, who could read their lips and the cruelty in their smiles, was fighting back the tears.

Barry, the owner of the shop, quickly came to the rescue. "They're jealous because they don't have your secret weapon," Barry said as he led Rosie into the office and tried to calm her down.

"What secret weapon?" Rosie sniffled.

"Your apple pie," he said with a serious look on his face.

"Stop it!" Rosie laughed as she wiped away the tears.

Barry was her best friend in the whole world. His string of would-be girlfriends couldn't understand why this drop-dead handsome man would bypass the most stylish and sophisticated ladies just to hang around Rosie's house and stretch out on her overstuffed sofa eating homemade apple pie. Rosie was not a trendy glamour queen. Instead she was a homespun, honey-colored Afro-centric lady who was a little on the plump side.

Rosie shared a secret bond with the successful and handsome Barry: Her hearing disability was on the outside where people could see. Barry's learning disability was on the inside and remained a secret that only he and Rosie shared.

His dyslexia had made him the object of ridicule as a child. But his strong determination was greater than his fears. He had moved to New York and found work as a model. After saving up enough money, he opened an upscale barbershop and beauty salon. But even as a grown man with a successful business, he still suffered from feelings of insecurity.

Rosie was a godsend. She managed the shop and took care of the bookkeeping and all of his other business matters. Because of her own struggles, she immediately recognized his. Over a period of time she gained his complete trust. She wanted his love but gladly settled for just being needed.

"I don't know what Barry sees in her," Sheila said to Connie as they sat under the dryers waiting for Barry to work his magic on their hair.

"Good help is hard to find," Connie laughed.

When it was time for Barry to style Sheila's hair, she strolled over to his chair like a runway model. "So, Barry, have you found a date for the big party at the Park Plaza?"

"Why? Do you have any suggestions?" he laughed.

"I'd be more than happy to come to your rescue," Sheila purred.

"Thanks for the offer, but I think I'll take Rosie out for a night on the town. She works so hard. It will be good for her to get out and let her hair down... Don't you agree?"

Sheila's body stiffened. "It's hard to imagine you going out on a date with Rosie...but that's what makes you special. You're so kindhearted and charitable."

As the two cat ladies were leaving the shop, Connie stopped by the desk to say good-bye to Rosie. "Have a good time at the charity ball, girl... If at all possible, look cute!"

"What ball?" Rosie looked confused.

"The one your boss is taking you to," she answered as she headed out the door.

At the end of the day Rosie finally worked up enough courage to ask Barry about Connie's comment. "What's this about a charity ball?" she casually mentioned.

"I almost forgot," Barry answered. "There's a big charity ball at the Park Plaza next week. Stevie Wonder is performing. I know how much you love Stevie, so I got the tickets."

"But I don't have anything to wear to a ball." Rosie was feeling anxious.

"I knew that's what you'd say. When you get home there should be a package waiting for you. I picked out something I think you would really love to wear."

Rosie's silence signaled Barry that something was wrong. "What? You don't want to go out with me?" He smiled.

"It's not that," Rosie said, looking away. "It's just that...well...I'm not very glamorous, and I don't want to embarrass you."

"Embarrass me? Don't you know that I'm who I am and where I am because of you? I'm so proud of you I could burst. You are one beautiful lady, and I can't wait to show you off."

Rosie was speechless. She walked over to Barry and gave him a big hug.

"Go home and open your box. Call me and let me know if it fits," Barry said.

Rosie was walking on air as she headed for home to get a look at the new dress Barry had picked for her to wear on their big night out. The special-delivery package was waiting for her when she walked in the door. Rosie's heart raced as she tore open the box. She wondered if Barry remembered that her favorite color was turquoise blue. Or maybe he picked a black dress to give her a more slender look.

When she opened the package, she was both shocked and confused. It was empty, except for a card and a small box—much too small for a dress. Rosie opened the card and began to read, thinking that perhaps this was one of Barry's practical jokes. His handwriting was barely legible: "My dearest Rose," the letter began. "As you know, I don't write very well. But I want you to know that I love you very much. I don't care what you wear to the ball. I just want you to marry me and stay with me forever. Love, Barry."

Rosie was in tears as she opened the small box and found the most beautiful engagement ring her eyes had ever seen.

"Yes, I'll marry you," she whispered to the empty room as she sat staring at the beautiful ring.

 God shall send forth His mercy and His truth.

PSALM 57:3

Chapter 9

The Beauty of Sapphire

A Woman of Prayer and Faith

> *Above the expanse over their heads was what*
> *looked like a throne of sapphire, and high above*
> *on the throne was a figure like that of a man.*
>
> EZEKIEL 1:26, NIV

The deep-blue sapphire is found in the fifth position on Aaron's breast-plate (see Exodus 28:18). Like its ruby sister, this royal jewel is second only to the diamond in hardness and brilliance. In ancient writings, the sapphire is often referred to as "the gem of heaven" or "the royal jewel." When God revealed himself to Moses and Ezekiel, the throne he sat upon and the floor under his feet were described as being made of "sapphire stone" (Exodus 24:10; Ezekiel 1:26).

The blue sapphire that adorned Aaron's breastplate, was inscribed with the name of Simeon, the second son born to Jacob and Leah (see Genesis 29:15-33). Leah had cried out in prayer to the Lord because she was unloved by her husband, Jacob. The Lord saw her pain, heard her cry, and answered her prayers. "When the LORD saw that Leah was unloved,

He opened her womb" (verse 31). She chose for her second son the name Simeon, which means "God hears" (see verse 33).

God indeed heard her cries. He gave Leah a total of six sons and one beautiful daughter. This woman is an example of God's miraculous response to prayers poured out in faith. In the midst of the pressure Leah faced in her marriage, prayer and faith became the centerpieces of her life.

In nine places in the Bible, the sapphire is acclaimed for its exceptional beauty. In addition to Aaron's breastplate and the throne of God, it also appears on the heavenly walls of the New Jerusalem (see Revelation 21:19). With all the beauty and glory ascribed to the sapphire, it is hard to believe that this gorgeous gemstone was twisted into a negative stereotype of Black women, popularized by the *Amos 'n' Andy* radio and television show. Now that we know the true beauty and honor the Bible attaches to the sapphire, we can embrace a new image and celebrate the New Sapphire, for we are shining examples of God's grace and glory.

The deep-blue sapphire stone acquired its beauty and strength from being buried under a mountain of pressure, and the same is true for the sapphire woman. The pressures of life shape her inner beauty. She knows the pressure of following her heart, even when it sets her apart from the people she loves. She knows the pressure of countless failures that ultimately lead to real success. She knows the pressure of fighting against the enemy within, the voice that says her best isn't good enough. But as she continues to endure, she will ultimately shine with the brilliance of a precious jewel.

As you consider the process of becoming a true sapphire, picture yourself digging into a gigantic mountain of dirt with a toy shovel. "What is the point?" you ask God. But despite the questions, doubts, and fears, you continue to dig because God compels you to follow his leading. You long to put down your shovel and walk away. A nagging voice inside says you are wasting your time, making a fool of yourself. But the powerful voice of faith sweetly reassures you that if you keep digging, your reward will come. When you least expect it, you plunge your tiny shovel into the ground and uncover a shining piece of blue rock. You pull it from the earth and wipe the dirt away, uncertain what you hold in your hands. You take your blue rock to a gemologist and learn you have uncovered a large, deep-blue sapphire. You can sell it and be wealthy.

You start to throw away your toy shovel, but the same voice that gave you the strength to keep digging before speaks now more clearly than ever, "Get a bigger shovel and dig deeper!"

No matter what plateau you've reached in your spiritual growth, there's always more to discover, more to achieve, more to reach for. Life is the mountain into which we are called to dig. Prayer is the shovel by which we uncover our destiny. Faith is the motivation that compels us to search for the treasure that is found by those who dare to believe.

The sapphire woman is birthed out of prayer and faith. Prayer involves not only having access to God but giving God access to us. Prayer is not only telling God what we want from him but listening to God so we will know what he wants from us. Faith is believing that we can achieve what God calls us to do, because with God all things are possible.

The man who wins the heart of a sapphire woman is blessed indeed. She will become a personal intercessor and bombard heaven on his behalf. When he is searching for the courage to take risks or move to a higher level, his shining sapphire queen will be there to stir his faith and whisper in his ear that he can do all things through Christ who strengthens him.

I wish I could give every Black woman in the world a sapphire ring to wear as a reminder to continue to walk in faith and pray deeply because "God hears." For those Black women who are still facing struggles, know that we all face challenges at one time or another. I encourage you to pick up your shovel and keep digging until you discover the treasure God has placed inside you. Continue to exercise faith and continue in prayer, knowing that your words will instantly reach the sapphire throne. Rest assured that God hears and will lead you to victory.

Hannah found herself buried under a mountain of grief as she listened to the joyful midwives who had just delivered a baby son to Peninnah, the second wife of her husband, Elkanah. "What a fine son you have," one of the nurses said to Elkanah. "You should be very proud of Peninnah. Truly, she is a fruitful vine."

In Hannah's world it was customary for a man to take a second wife if his first was barren. Hannah's husband loved her deeply, but when the relationship failed to produce children, Elkanah had married Peninnah, who soon gave birth to a son and then a daughter—and then more sons, including this latest addition to the family.

As she listened to the women cooing over the baby, Hannah entertained two visitors, Anger and Jealousy. Anger spoke first inside Hannah's heart: "Why do you bother to pray and have faith that God will hear you when Peninnah, who neither prays nor has faith, is clearly receiving all the blessings?"

Jealousy quickly added to the conversation: "Elkanah says he loves you now, but Peninnah is the woman who is giving him children. It won't be long before she takes your place in his heart."

Hannah hurt deeply at the thought of losing her husband's love and never giving him children.

Elkanah knew the source of Hannah's pain and shared her grief. With or without children, he loved Hannah more than Peninnah or anyone on earth. He gave her everything she desired, but he could not give her children. Elkanah tried to find words to comfort her. "Hannah…why is your heart grieved? Am I not better to you than ten sons?"

Through the years she would hear these words many times. But Elkanah's words could not shield her from Peninnah's mocking glares. Nor could his love protect her from the women of her village who pitied her for being cursed with barrenness.

In the midst of her suffering, Hannah found one small consolation. With each day of prayer, a peace came upon her that surpassed all understanding. Each time she asked the Lord to take away her barrenness and give her a son, the seed of faith was watered, took root, and grew.

When the time came for Hannah and her husband to travel to the city of Shiloh for the yearly worship, Hannah trembled as she entered the temple. A fire burned in her heart. She tried her best to contain the powerful emotions stirring within her, but soon the floodgates opened wide and she was lost in a whirlwind of worship and prayer. Elkanah, along with Peninnah and her children, waited for Hannah to finish. But when they saw no end to her lifted hands, falling tears, swaying body, and moving lips, they left her alone with the Lord.

As the sun faded from the sky and the temple emptied of people, Hannah spiraled deeper and deeper into prayer. Her soul ascended into the heavens to approach the sapphire throne of God. She lay stretched out before the Lord, refusing to leave his holy presence until he answered the cry of her heart: "Lord, give me a son…please, Lord, give me a son. If you give me a son, I vow that I will give him back to you." Whether she spoke within herself, or was screaming out loud, she could not tell.

But she did not stop praying, begging, pleading with God until he answered. "Yes, I will give you a son!"

Hannah was unspeakably joyful as she returned from the mysterious heavenly place. Lying on the steps of the temple, she staggered to her feet, but the intoxication of praise and thanksgiving caused her to collapse again and again.

Hannah embraced her husband with passion and expectation. Soon she was pregnant and gave birth to a son, just as God had promised. The child was as strong and beautiful as her unshakable faith. She called the child Shemu'el, which translates to Samuel, and in Hebrew means "I have asked and God hears."

Hannah's story, adapted from 1 Samuel 1, reveals the life-changing power of heartfelt prayer. The woman of African ancestry who knows how to exercise faith and touch the throne of God in prayer possesses the strength and beauty of a brilliant sapphire. God hears her prayers not because of eloquent or fiery words, but because she lives a life of faith and comes before the throne of God in prayer.

History demonstrates that in the arena of prayer and faith, God has a special affection for women of African descent. Some of the difficulties we presently face cannot be compared to those of our ancestors. From the days of the slave traders to the Civil Rights movement, God has heard the prayers of Black women, and he has given us the strength to overcome every obstacle.

Women who live by prayer and faith have shaped the history of Black people around the world. Educator Mary McLeod Bethune is one of my favorite examples of a woman who used the tools of prayer and faith to achieve her goals. In 1875 Mary McLeod Bethune was born in South Carolina into a family of seventeen children. Her parents were former slaves. Mary endured the racism and the poverty of the Reconstruction era only by prayer and faith.

Mary became an outstanding student at the Presbyterian Mission School, which had been established in her county to teach the freed slaves and their children how to read and write. During this time she also learned scriptures about the power of prayer and faith. In spite of her meager circumstances, she believed that one day she would become a missionary to Africa. Her family and friends thought her dream was impossible, but Mary remained strong in her faith and in her desire to serve God.

With the help of the Lord, Mary broke new ground as an African American: She attended Scotia Seminary and graduated from Moody Bible Institute. But with every obstacle she overcame, a new one came to take its place. In spite of her determination to become a missionary to Africa, the White missionary society rejected her application because of her race. Mary was deeply wounded, but she never abandoned hope, and she continued in prayer and faith.

Eventually, God heard. She was led by the Lord to become a missionary to Black girls in America. At the turn of the century, she organized the Daytona Literary and Industrial School for Training Negro Girls. In 1923 the school merged with the Cookman Institute and eventually became known as Bethune-Cookman College.

Mary McLeod Bethune served as president of the college for almost forty years. She also became the founder of the National Council of Negro Women and served as an educational advisor to President Harry Truman.

Two important lessons can be learned from the story of Mary McLeod Bethune. First, by prayer we gain purpose and direction from God. Second, by faith we find the courage to follow where God leads.

I have observed that unlike Peter, who willingly stepped out of the boat and walked on water, Black women walk on water because they don't have a boat and there's no time or money for swimming lessons! Dealing with the pressures of life, Black women have learned how to effectively utilize the tools of prayer and faith.

The following keys will further unlock the power of prayer and increase your faith as a sapphire woman.

SEVEN PRINCIPLES OF EFFECTIVE PRAYER

1. Pray for your enemies and forgive them.

And whenever you stand praying, if you have anything against anyone, forgive him, that your Father in heaven may also forgive you your trespasses. (Mark 11:25)

2. Pray confessing your sins.

Therefore confess your sins to each other and pray for each other so that you may be healed. The prayer of a righteous man is powerful and effective. (James 5:16, NIV)

3. Pray in agreement with others.

Again I say to you that if two of you agree on earth concerning anything that they ask, it will be done for them by My Father in heaven. (Matthew 18:19)

4. Pray and fast.

But when you fast, put oil on your head and wash your face, so that it will not be obvious to men that you are fasting, but only to your Father, who is unseen; and your Father, who sees what is done in secret, will reward you. (Matthew 6:17-18, NIV)

5. Pray in righteousness.

For the eyes of the LORD are on the righteous
and His ears are open to their prayers. (1 Peter 3:12)

6. Pray in private.

But when you pray, go into your room, close the door and pray to your Father, who is unseen. Then your Father, who sees what is done in secret, will reward you. (Matthew 6:6, NIV)

7. Pray in the Spirit.

Praying always with all prayer and supplication in the Spirit, being watchful to this end with all perseverance and supplication for all the saints. (Ephesians 6:18)

SEVEN STEPS TO BUILDING FAITH

1. Believe that by faith we are saved.

For by grace you have been saved through faith, and that not of yourselves; it is the gift of God. (Ephesians 2:8)

2. Believe that if you have faith, whatever need you ask in prayer, the need will be met.

Assuredly, I say to you, if you have faith and do not doubt…whatever things you ask in prayer, believing, you will receive. (Matthew 21:21-22)

3. Believe by faith that obstacles blocking your progress will be moved.

If you have faith as a mustard seed, you will say to this mountain, "Move from here to there," and it will move; and nothing will be impossible for you. (Matthew 17:20)

4. Believe that good works are the evidence of real faith.

Show me your faith without your works, and I will show you my faith by my works. (James 2:18)

5. Believe that faith is a key to healing and deliverance.

And [Jesus] said to her, "Daughter, be of good cheer; your faith has made you well." (Luke 8:48)

6. Believe that faith moves us to take extreme action.

Because of the crowd, they uncovered the roof where [Jesus] was. So when they had broken through, they let down the bed on

which the paralytic was lying. When Jesus saw their faith,
He said to the paralytic, "Son, your sins are forgiven you."
(Mark 2:4)

7. Believe that faith gives us power to withstand the attacks
    of Satan.

Above all, taking the shield of faith with which you will be able
to quench all the fiery darts of the wicked one. (Ephesians 6:16)

Cleo opened her dresser drawer and stared at the brown envelope that
contained her monthly welfare check. By now she had lost count of the
number of times she had looked at the check and tried to make the one
decision that would permanently take her to a new level of faith. She
gripped the check tightly and struggled against the fear that was holding
her back. Finally with one swift jerk, she ripped it in half.

Her heart was racing as she sat down on the side of her sagging bed.
"What have I done? I must be losing my mind!" Cleo mumbled to herself
as she looked at the torn pieces of brown paper. She picked up her Bible
and held it against her chest and tried to pray.

"Here you are with no husband and three kids to feed and you're tearing up your welfare check," the voice of doubt spoke from within. "Are
you trying to tell God that the check he provided for you isn't good
enough? Is that it?"

In spite of the thoughts swirling around in her mind, Cleo opened the
pages of her Bible and read the words that inspired her to put her faith

into action. "What is faith? It is the confident assurance that something we want is going to happen" (Hebrews 11:1, TLB).

As she considered those words, Cleo thought back to five years ago when she had been secretly working in a sewing factory to make extra money. The owner of the rundown establishment agreed to pay her cash under the table and to rotate her hours so her social worker wouldn't find out that she was working part time. Cleo knew that she was breaking the law, but playing by the welfare rules meant that she would have to depend solely on the monthly check and food stamps, and she knew from experience that wasn't enough. She also knew that even if she got off welfare and worked full time at her factory job, it wouldn't pay enough to take care of herself and her children. Raymond, her children's father, helped her out from time to time, but his part-time job in a potato chip factory paid so little that it left him too embarrassed to face his children on a regular basis. So Cleo did what she had to do.

She had no hope that her life would ever change, so she set her sights on coping rather than hoping. Then her ten-year-old son Ray started attending an after-school Bible program at a nearby church.

"I'm gonna be an astronaut!" Ray Jr. announced one day as he sat in front of the television watching a space program.

Cleo sat across from him folding clothes. "You ain't gonna be nothing!" She instantly regretted her words, but she had just finished working a double shift at the factory. She was dead tired, and the money she earned was already owed to cover loans she had taken out the month before.

Ray wasn't the least bit bothered by what she said. His response caught her completely off guard. "I am going to be something! 'Cause I can do all things through Christ who strengthens me!" He looked at Cleo with a bold assurance she had never before seen in him, and she certainly didn't understand its source.

"Where did you get that?" She looked at him while trying to hide her confusion.

"From the Bible," Ray grinned.

"What do you know about the Bible?" Cleo taunted.

Ray could barely contain his excitement. "I read the Bible every day. My teacher says that if I have the faith, God has the power. That's how I know I'm going to be an astronaut, 'cause I got faith!" Ray held up his blue paperback student edition of the Holy Bible.

"Let me see that." Cleo reached over and picked up the book, which looked nothing like the Bibles she was accustomed to seeing. The cover featured pictures of kids on skateboards and bikes, and the words inside were in everyday English.

For the next few hours the basket of clothes remained unfolded and the dinner remained uncooked as Cleo read through the pages. A passage from the book of Hebrews caught her attention and refused to let go. "What is faith? It is the confident assurance that something we want is going to happen" (Hebrews 11:1a, TLB).

A light came on inside Cleo's head as she continued to read. "It is the certainty that what we hope for is waiting for us, even though we cannot see it up ahead" (Hebrews 11:1b, TLB).

That's how Cleo's journey of faith began. Over and over she read through the blue Bible with skateboards and bicycles on the cover. Finally, she purchased her own copy and started attending the neighborhood church.

"Where did you get a sewing machine?" her children asked on the day she set up her power machine in the living room.

"Faith!" Cleo winked at Ray.

At first Cleo didn't think her sewing was anything special. But more and more women from her neighborhood and her church were placing orders for dresses, suits, and Easter frocks for their children.

Her business grew steadily, but even though she had given her heart to the Lord, she still didn't have the courage to let go of the security that she found in her welfare check. The Lord understood the fear she was feeling. Someone once referred to the process of change as "walking naked in the land of uncertainty."*

Once again her son Ray offered the bit of courage she needed to take the next step. For the first time in his life he got an A in math on his report card.

"How in the world did you raise your grade from a D to an A?" Cleo asked.

"'Cause I'm going to be an astronaut. And astronauts have to be good in math."

That was a turning point in Cleo's life. She started having dreams that filled her heart with a mixture of fear and excitement. She dreamed of designing her own clothing line and having her own factory. But she certainly wasn't dreaming when she quit her part-time job and could barely handle the list of customers in her dressmaking business.

Cleo sat on the edge of the bed, reflecting on all that had happened and looking at the torn-up pieces of her final welfare check. The tears rolled down her face as she whispered her prayer: "Lord, please don't play with me! What am I going to do if you don't help me? Do you know how many people have let me down in my life?"

---

* R. E. Quinn, *Deep Change: Discovering the Leader Within* (San Francisco: Jossey-Bass, 1996), 36.

Most people don't believe that God can speak to us just like a real person, but on that day Cleo could hear his voice loud and clear: "Have faith, Cleo. Very soon, you're going to have your own clothing factory and your oldest son will travel into the heavens."

When Cleo told her social worker that she and her children no longer needed welfare, the woman responded, "Whatever you're up to, just make sure that your kids don't end up in foster care because you're doing jail time."

The sting of the woman's words caught Cleo off guard for a moment, but she quickly recovered and stood to her feet. "You've got it all wrong," Cleo smiled at her social worker. "Welfare is jail time, but my faith in God has set me free!"

Now the just shall live by faith;
But if anyone draws back,
My soul has no pleasure in him.

Hebrews 10:38

Chapter 10

The Beauty of Diamond

A Woman of Strength and Prosperity

Strength and honor are her clothing;
She shall rejoice in time to come.

PROVERBS 31:25

The diamond occupies the sixth position on Aaron's breastplate and is inscribed with the name Gad, the son of Zilpah, the maid of Leah. Gad rose from lowly beginnings to prominence among the twelve brothers.

Leah called Zilpah's son Gad, which means "a troop comes" (see Genesis 30:11). The name also means "good fortune." On Aaron's breastplate, the brilliance and strength of the diamond reflect good fortune and Gad's strong, shining personality. When Jacob pronounced a final blessing over his twelve sons, he said of Gad, "A troop shall tramp upon him, but he shall triumph at last" (Genesis 49:19). Some say a diamond is nothing more than a piece of carbon that could take the heat. So too, Gad faced tremendous pressure and persecution—and always prevailed.

In Deuteronomy, Moses portrayed Gad as a warrior who would ultimately destroy his enemies and enjoy the rewards that come with victory. When Moses pronounced a blessing over the tribe of Gad he said, "Blessed is he who enlarges Gad's domain! Gad lives there like a lion, tearing at arm or head. He chose the best land for himself; the leader's portion was kept for him. When the heads of the people assembled, he carried out the LORD'S righteous will, and his judgments concerning Israel" (Deuteronomy 33:20-21, NIV)

King David described the men of the tribe of Gad as fearless soldiers, fierce and warlike. "Some from the tribe of Gad joined David. Their faces were like lions, and they were as swift as gazelles on the mountain" (see 1 Chronicles 12:8, my paraphrase).

No one is more fearless than a diamond woman. Just as the ruby woman ushers in praise and the woman of sapphire stirs faith, our diamond girlfriend brings courage and strength to the fainthearted.

Some Black women were born to shine. Their personalities light up the room when they enter it. Others possess a quiet dignity. They don't light up a room, but you can feel their power when you are in their presence. Whether they have a radiant personality or quiet dignity, both are cut from the same stone. Both are attributes of the most valuable jewel in the world, the diamond.

Ladies with diamonds in their souls thrive on challenges and grow stronger with every victory. No matter how many times these sisters get pushed off the ladder, they start climbing all over again. It appears that good fortune is on their side, and despite challenges, the Lord grants diamond ladies his choicest blessings.

As a child, the diamond was never afraid to take risks. She was the born leader, always talking her brothers, sisters, and friends into participating in crazy schemes. She was so bright her teachers could not ignore her, and her parents had to be tough to keep this little girl in check.

She grew into a jewel of a woman who views obstacles as a staircase to be climbed to reach her destiny. She is successful. She is clear about what she stands for and what she believes in. Envy and jealousy sniff at her heels like bloodhounds, but before you join the posse of diamond haters, know that her strength and good fortune are no accident. God made her the pick of the litter. The diamondlike woman is more than a pretty face or a successful career. She has endured more heat, pressure, and tough times than any other jewel. That is the real source of her strength and beauty. That is what makes her stronger than any other jewel that God created.

I have seen this diamondlike spirit in Black girls who grew up in drug-infested neighborhoods in America and in the economically forgotten countryside of the Caribbean Islands. No matter how bad their circumstances, they are determined to find a way out of poverty and despair. In South Africa, I talked to young women whose eyes sparkled like diamonds. They served in the national anti-apartheid movement and now are struggling for personal victories. Because of their strength and because God is on their side, these young ladies will become the next generation of leaders in South Africa. But like any true diamond, their transition into that role will not come without great effort.

Just as diamonds are buried so deep in the earth that it takes a volcanic eruption to spew them to the surface, upheavals in our personal lives bring our diamond qualities to the surface. The diamond lady is not an overnight sensation. It takes time and testing for her to develop the power that causes her to shine brightly in the darkest situation.

A Black woman who is like a genuine diamond develops in ways that parallel the mining of African diamonds. Many human rights organizations refer to diamonds mined in Africa as "conflict diamonds," referring to rebels who take over diamond mines and sell the stones to purchase weapons for liberation. African diamonds are also known as "blood diamonds" because the workers in the mines suffer abuse of every kind.

Diamond earrings, tennis bracelets, and engagement rings are often produced with the blood of African workers. In South Africa, Angola, and the Republic of Congo, Black people are brutalized, displaced, and murdered by hired guns from diamond companies, rebels, and governments who seek to control the production of these precious gems. The greedy and ungodly have stripped billions of dollars in diamonds from African soil with no compensation to African people. Even with the end of apartheid in South Africa, mine workers go without medical care, live in squalor, and are still paid as little as twenty-five dollars a month for working sixteen-hour days. The workers often lose their lives in the deplorable, slavelike conditions of the African diamond mines.

Diamonds that could have transformed Africa into a rich and prosperous continent fell into the hands of men like Cecil Rhodes, cofounder of the DeBeers Mining Company. History records that Rhodes became one of the richest men of his day after swindling Lobengula, king of what was then Matabeleland, out of a vast diamond-rich territory in southern Africa. Rhodes renamed the region Rhodesia. Today he is remembered for creating the Rhodes Scholarships of Oxford University, but his wealth was built from the exploitation of others.

Just as many diamonds are harvested in conflict and oppression, Black women have been born and grown up in such circumstances. Diamond women remain unbreakable, their true value never changes, and the injustices only make them stronger and shinier.

My dear friend Pat Ashley possesses the personality of a diamond. She's a take-charge lady who shines with strength and finesse. Blessings seem to follow her wherever she goes. When I was facing a great challenge in my life, I called her for prayer. With words of confidence and spiritual authority she said to me, "Don't let the devil see you sweat! Get dressed, curl your hair, fix your face, and ride out the storm with style. You already know that the Lord will give you the victory. You know that the situation you're facing will build your faith, make you stronger and wiser."

You may be a diamond, not yet cut or fully polished. Know that you have great value and be careful not to allow yourself to fall into the wrong hands. Ungodly people can recognize your value even when you can't. If you are not wise you will be deceived and misused. "Above all else, guard your heart, for it is the wellspring of life" (Proverbs 4:23, NIV).

The caravan made its way across the desert, a spectacular serpent slithering over sloping hills and through deep canyons of golden sand. The camels, heavy laden with priceless cargo, were destined for Solomon, son of David, king of Israel. From the land of Sheba to the city of Jerusalem, the magnificent parade made its journey loaded with enough spices to sweeten the air of an entire city. Flawless jewels of every color, size, and shape filled the leather pouches.

Legions of soldiers carefully guarded a special procession of bejeweled camels that carried sacks of pure gold. Even more closely guarded was the chariot that carried the queen of Sheba, the bearer of these gifts for Solomon.

The heat and dust penetrated the queen's veil and filled her nostrils with the dry stench of sand and sweaty human flesh. No amount of sweetened wine or fanning handmaidens brought relief from the heat of the sun. But this time of suffering and inconvenience was a necessary sacrifice for this Ethiopian queen, who hoped to establish a trade agreement with King Solomon.

The king sent his royal guard and a host of musicians and singers miles outside the city walls of Jerusalem to welcome the caravan and escort the queen to the palace. Inside the royal chambers a cool mist of scented water continuously filled the air. Marble pillars and floors framed the rooms, and linen drapes of the softest blue, threaded with silver and gold, hung from the walls and ceilings. A tapestry bearing her royal crest covered a bed of hand-carved ivory overlaid with gold. The queen smiled with approval.

After a long bath she stretched her bronze body across the luxurious bed and rehearsed her plan. King Solomon held key control of the trade routes, and even though her country was rich in produce and spices, she needed his favor to continue to move her caravans freely through the territories that led to the lands of Africa, India, and Arabia.

Her heart fluttered at the thought of meeting Solomon face to face. The wise men of her court had repeated many of Solomon's proverbs and told stories of his great wealth and his collection of beautiful wives and concubines. She prayed that she would find favor with this mighty king and win access to trade routes without war.

King Solomon paced back and forth waiting for his cupbearer and scribe. This mysterious ruler from the south weighed heavily on his mind. The stories he'd heard about her were too astonishing to be true. He wondered how one fragile woman could produce such great wealth and why both kings and common slaves esteemed her so highly. She seemed more mythical than real. Stories of her flawless African beauty reminded Solomon of his own weaknesses when it came to women. If this queen was as lovely as she was brilliant, he would have to carefully guard his heart.

"What does a woman know about trade?" he said out loud as his cupbearer entered the room, followed by his scribe.

The cupbearer bowed and then looked up at King Solomon, awaiting permission to speak. Solomon nodded. "The queen of Sheba is more prosperous than all of the kings of the south. Her spice trade alone is worth a fortune in gold."

"Is she as beautiful as they say?" Solomon asked.

The cupbearer smiled. "I had an audience with her this morning your majesty. My eyes will never be the same."

King Solomon gave his approval on the final preparation for the banquet to take place the following evening. He also ordered his wives and concubines to be present. He was certain that this ruler of the south could never surpass his collection of wives.

But when the queen of Sheba made her entrance, they all paled in comparison to this flawless jewel. Shimmering light seemed to surround her as she stood before Solomon, arrayed in splendor. She held out a small golden box.

"Indeed the half was not told me. Your wisdom and prosperity exceed the fame of which I heard," she said to the king. Sweetly, she handed him the small gold box. Solomon could not contain his pleasure as he opened it and removed a perfectly cut diamond ring, especially crafted and engraved for the king.

"Everyone leave us!" Solomon raised his hand. When the room was empty, the king rose and, taking the queen by her hand, led her to a tapestry cushion next to his own. He could not stop staring at her glistening eyes and perfectly chiseled features.

She smiled as Solomon bowed before her like a humble servant and said, "Whatever you command I will obey, for I am now your slave."

"Blessed be the LORD your God, who delighted in you, setting you on the throne of Israel!" She paused for a moment and continued, "I beg that you would tell me the source of your great wisdom. And later I would like to talk about trade."

And King Solomon gave the queen of Sheba all that she desired and whatever she asked.

The man who falls in love with a diamond lady must be self-assured. An insecure man might find himself intimidated by her charisma and strength. If he aspires to a life of success and prominence, the diamond lady will be a jewel in his crown. She has beauty, smarts, and endurance. Most of all, in good times and in bad times, she will never stop shining.

We can learn much from the account in 1 Kings 10 of the queen of Sheba's visit to King Solomon's court, from which the preceding story was adapted. Let me point out a few nuggets of wisdom that deserve our attention.

Have a plan for your life. The queen of Sheba wasn't acting on a whim; she had a serious plan to present to King Solomon. If you don't know where you're going, or you don't have a plan for your life, you probably won't reach a worthwhile destination.

Seek spiritual truths. Scripture makes it clear that the queen of Sheba was in search of spiritual wisdom and viewed Solomon as a wise teacher. First Kings 10:3 says Solomon answered all of her questions; nothing was too difficult for the king to explain to her. A woman seeking wisdom will find it.

Have your own stuff. Dr. Renita Weems, an author and educator, tells Black women who want to share the company of great men not to show up empty handed. If you want the best, then be the best! The queen of Sheba did not come to Solomon's court begging for anything. She had her own stuff.

Have a teachable spirit. The queen of Sheba gained knowledge and wisdom by asking questions and listening carefully. She said little about herself.

Have a humble spirit. "Men are not intimidated by what a woman has, but by how she brings it to the table." That advice came from Patricia Ashley. It is better to be humble and gracious than to be an arrogant Black woman. The queen of Sheba was never haughty about her wealth and trade savvy. Her achievements spoke for her.

Be kind, gracious, and generous. The queen of Sheba proved that your gifts will make room for you and bring you before kings (see Proverbs 18:16). A gracious and generous woman will always benefit in the end.

Look good at all times. Diamonds are placed in great settings because of their value. Respect who you are and what the Lord has placed in you by dressing in a classy manner. Dr. Myles Monroe has said that your dress determines how you are addressed.

The smell of sickness filled the stately bedroom as the man with the pale, twisted faced railed at the two women standing at the foot of his bed. The lovely woman with her hair pulled back in a silver French roll trembled with embarrassment.

"Tell Lolo how you crawled out of the gutter and tricked me into marrying you." The depraved man raised his head from the pillow gasping for air as he glared first at his trusted housekeeper, Lolo, and then at Dora, his wife of forty years.

"No one in the whole of South Africa knows the truth about you, but I know what you really are!" He pointed his disjointed finger at Dora.

Dora sobbed as she buried her delicate face in the arms of Lolo. "The doctor said it will all be over soon," Lolo whispered words of comfort.

Lolo hadn't seen her own house in days, but she couldn't leave Dora alone with this dying man whose fury made him like someone possessed by an evil spirit.

As the evening wore on, the two women sat together in the sick room watching over the dying man. Dora quietly prayed while Lolo read her Bible.

When Dora finished praying, Lolo whispered, "You know I'll be gone for a few hours tomorrow morning."

Dora sighed. "Yes, I know. For the one hundredth time: Tomorrow is Molano's big race and you want to be there. I'll be right here praying for him to win."

Lolo looked concerned. "Please, let my sister come stay with you tomorrow."

"I'll be fine, Lolo. All dear Henry can do is rant and rave. He's too weak to get out of bed." Dora affectionately touched Lolo's hand. "I'm so proud of Molano. Who would have thought such a skinny boy from Soweto would be the favorite in the South African marathon."

A look of joy and sadness came together in Lolo's eyes. "How I wish his father could have lived long enough to see this day. When he was alive, each day he'd come home from the diamond mines and say the same thing to Molano: 'Boy, you're just like the diamond mines. You don't look like much on the outside, but something of real value is buried inside you. One day you're going to be somebody!' "

Dora looked straight into Lolo's eyes and began to whisper. "The story that you're telling about Molano and his father…well, I want to share something with you that I've never told anyone in my entire life."

Dora took a deep breath. Her lips began to tremble as she spoke. "I'm not the woman you think I am, Lolo. You see, my mother was White and my father was colored, but he looked almost White. That's how they were able to marry."

Dora looked at Lolo, expecting her to be shocked. But Lolo had already heard parts of the story in the delirious ravings of Dora's cancer-ridden husband. She looked down at the floor as she continued her story. It was as if she were finally releasing a burden that she had carried for much too long.

"My parents came to Johannesburg from a small town near Cape Coast. They were dirt poor, but my daddy always said, 'Dora, you're not going to live in poverty all your life. You're going to be somebody.' I worked hard and saved up enough money to go to business school. God forgive me, but things were so bad for Coloreds and Blacks that I had to pass for White to get a job working as a secretary. That's how I met Henry. He was older and very rich, and he never dreamed that I had Black blood in my veins.

"I guess one thing led to another. He was the man of my dreams, so when I had a chance to marry him I took it."

"How did he find out that you were colored?" Lolo asked.

Dora smiled. "I finally told him the truth. I just couldn't keep living a lie. I told him he could get an annulment, but I guess he was too in love or too proud to go through with it. He just grew distant and bitter over the years. But still, at times, he would forget all about our secret and shower me with so much love and affection that I could hardly contain it all.

"Then something would trigger his hatred against Black people—an uprising at the mines or the sight of a mixed couple walking along the street. For a long time he would treat me like I wasn't even alive, then it would pass."

Lolo didn't speak. She laid her hand on Dora's shoulder and prayed from the deepest recesses of her heart. When she finished she looked at her dear friend. "The Lord is going to work things out. You'll see," Lolo whispered.

The night passed and the next morning Lolo left for her son's race. As expected Molano finished in first place, and the prize money was enough to fulfill his dream of going to college far away from the racism of South Africa.

It was almost dark when Lolo returned to Dora's house. She found her employer and friend sitting by her husband's lifeless body.

"Did Molano win his race?" Dora never stopped looking at Henry.

"Yes, he did," Lolo said softly.

A long silence filled the room, then Dora spoke again. "I won my race too. Before Henry died, he asked me to forgive him for the way he treated me. He told me that he loved me and that I was worth more than all the diamonds in the world."

"Thank the Lord," Lolo whispered. "Thank the Lord."

Dora's voice was trembling. "I have something for Molano. I want him to have Henry's jewelry chest of diamond cuff links, rings, tiepins, and watches. I left it on the dresser for you to take to him. It's a perfect gift for a young man who will be very successful one day."

"I believe he will," Lolo said. Her eyes filled with tears as she opened the jewelry box. Never before in her life had she seen so many diamonds.

"Henry left me his entire estate, Lolo. Perhaps I'll use the money to build schools in the townships, so that the African children can get a better education. At last the good Lord has made a way for me to help my own people."

"My prayers have been answered," Lolo said as she took one last look at Henry's lifeless body. The angry lines that once covered his face were replaced with the look of a man who was at peace with God.

And we know that all things work together
for good to those who love God, to those who
are the called according to His purpose.

ROMANS 8:28

Chapter 11

The Beauty of Opal

A Woman of Dreams and Fruitfulness

Our sister, may you increase to thousands upon thousands;
may your offspring possess the gates of their enemies.

GENESIS 24:60, NIV

The fiery opal is found in the seventh position on Aaron's breastplate, engraved with the name of Ephraim. In some writings, however, Joseph is listed in the seventh position.

You may already know the story in Genesis 37 of Joseph and how Jacob honored this son above all the others because he was the first child born to Rachel, the wife he truly loved. Even though Jacob did not know that a time would come when Joseph would save his people, he recognized that Joseph had a special anointing from the Lord. In his younger years, his father made him a coat of many colors. It was a valuable garment, usually worn by those of royal birth. It caused Joseph to be as vulnerable as a brightly colored opal.

Joseph also resembled a fragile opal as he openly exposed his dreams to the light. His shining moment—revealing the dream that he would one day reign over his brothers—brought him great harm. When Joseph told his brothers about his dream, it fueled their jealousy. They plotted to kill him, but Reuben argued for his life. The brothers sold him to slave traders who took him to the land of Egypt. In this place of adversity, being a dreamer brought Joseph wealth and power.

Years later, Joseph was reunited with his father and brothers. In a display of affection for his eleventh son, Jacob formally adopted Joseph's two children, Ephraim and Manasseh (see Genesis 48:5).

Ephraim replaced his father, Joseph, as head of one of the twelve tribes of Israel. His brother Manasseh replaced Levi because the tribes of Levi (known as the Levites) were set aside for the priesthood. Therefore, as we look at the seventh jewel on Aaron's breastplate, we must consider Joseph as well as Ephraim, whose name means "double fruitfulness." Joseph gave him the name because the Lord had allowed him and his children to prosper in the land of Egypt. The characteristics of these two men—dreams and fruitfulness—are symbolized by the fragile and colorful opal.

The beautiful opal is the most delicate of all jewels. Too much exposure to light, heat, or pressure will cause it to dry out and crack into pieces. If mishandled, it is easily chipped or broken. Opals sparkle with a rainbow of colors, and black opals—the most valuable of these gems—offer the most brilliant color display. The fireworks of its color can be seen clearly against the dark backdrop: red for sacrifice, green for increase, purple for royalty, and gold for endurance. In ancient times, the Romans called the opal "anchor of hope" because its multiple colors might appear darker in one instance but much lighter and brighter in another setting. The opal reminded the wearer that, no matter how bad things appeared at the moment, they would change as time passed.

The Black woman who is an opal dares to be a dreamer. Her visions help her soar like a bird that flies above every obstacle to reach her destiny.

She dreams with her eyes wide open. Her thinking is unique and original; her ideas are creative, like an opal jewel that displays unique prism shapes and colors.

The colorful opal woman has the gift of relating to all types of people. She has a variety of friends and acquaintances. In spiritual matters, she is a true ambassador of the Lord. When she walks into a room, people of all backgrounds are drawn to her; she is a natural people-person. Lady opal is a master at encouraging the weak, supporting the strong, and drawing shy people out of their shells. A little opal in all of us would make the world a friendlier place.

A Black lady opal is determined to fulfill her destiny. She has an inner anchor of hope that keeps her holding on until her dream becomes a reality. She refuses to be discouraged by racial discrimination, gender exclusion, or any other challenge. Opal women are often found among those who make discoveries or create a new way of doing things. They are "onlies" and "firsts"—the only Black woman to achieve a certain goal or the pioneer Blacks in a particular endeavor.

However, like Joseph, a Black woman who is a dreamer can arouse fear and jealousy, especially in cultures where her dreams are not encouraged and nurtured. Many Black inventors, scientists, musicians, and artists saw their dreams crushed or stolen by those who practiced oppression and racism. Poet Phillis Wheatley was the first Black woman to publish a book in America. But this gifted poet died in poverty.

In 1951, Bessie Blount was a nurse working with veterans of World War II. She invented a device that allowed the disabled and amputees to feed themselves through an automated tube. She proved that her invention worked, but the American medical community tried to crush her idea. She finally turned over her patent to the French government, and her invention was mass-produced for hospitals around the world.

In spite of many obstacles, the Lord often has made a way for women of African ancestry to realize their dreams. In the past and in the present, Black women inventors made discoveries, great and small, that changed the world and demonstrated the miracle-working power of God.

Many of these opal women first saw their inventions in dreams and visions. Millionaire businesswoman Madam C. J. Walker wrote that after much prayer she dreamed of a man who stood before her holding in his hand a formula that she later developed into a hair-care product.

The idea that one man's trash is a Black woman's treasure sparked the creativity of women like Clara Frye, who invented surgical instruments from scrap metal.

Even before women of African ancestry were allowed to pursue higher education, they found a way to give birth to their dreams. Armed with God-given brilliance and wisdom, the following brave dreamers were instrumental in creating the future:

Alice Parker. In 1919, she invented the first furnace that provided central heating for homes. The thermostat and special ducts controlled the heat in individual rooms.

Sarah Goode. In 1885, Sarah, who owned a Chicago furniture store, invented the fold-up hideaway bed. She was also the first African-American woman to receive a U.S. patent.

Sarah Boone. In 1892, she invented an ironing board with a narrow tip that allowed for ironing the narrow parts of shirts and dresses.

Bertha Berman. In 1959, this woman introduced the world to the first fitted sheets, which she had designed and patented.

Henrietta Bradberry. In 1945, this housewife invented the thrust mechanism for underwater torpedoes that were used on submarines.

Marjorie Joyner. In 1928, she invented the permanent wave machine, a hair perming device that was used for many years by both White and

Black women. She was an employee of Madame C. J. Walker, who invented the first Black hair-care products.

Dr. Patricia Bath. In 1988, she invented a laser device for removing cataracts, which transformed eye surgery worldwide. With another invention, Dr. Bath was able to restore sight to people who had been blind for over thirty years. She graduated from Howard University Medical School and became the first woman professor at UCLA Eye Institute.

Dr. Shirley Ann Jackson. Between 1975 and 1978, she worked for AT&T and developed the touch-tone telephone, portable fax, solar cell phone, and optic cables used in overseas telephone calls. In 1995 she was appointed chairwoman of the Nuclear Regulatory Commission for the United States government. She was also the first African American to receive a Ph.D. from Massachusetts Institute of Technology.

Scripture tells us that the wisdom that comes from relationship with God can open our imagination to a whole new realm of creativity. "I wisdom dwell with prudence, and find out knowledge of witty inventions" (Proverbs 8:12, KJV). An opal woman knows how to transform her God-given dreams into fruitful enterprises.

Lydia tried her best to ignore the feeling of loneliness. She had traveled around the world and purchased everything her heart desired, but her efforts to find happiness proved futile. After losing her husband at an early age, she hoped once again to find love and contentment with someone new. But instead, she only found more heartache.

To ease her pain, Lydia poured herself into the business of selling purple dye. After a lot of hard work and trial and error, Lydia developed a secret formula for crimson and deep purple dyes that would lock onto any fabric and never lose their brilliance. Throughout the Greek provinces, dye makers and linen weavers bowed to Lydia's achievements. She was the most successful businesswoman in the city of Philippi—and also the loneliest.

Her house was a splendid palace, but for Lydia it was more like a tomb. People surrounded her and cared deeply for her, but she felt lonely and unloved. Others obeyed her every wish, but she felt powerless.

One of her faithful servants recognized Lydia's discontent and introduced her to the Jewish faith. Lydia was searching for anything to fill the void in her life, so she willingly embraced the religion. She prayed and studied the Scriptures and did all in her power to keep God's law. But as time passed, she again felt the void in her life.

One Sabbath morning as Lydia sat by the river's edge praying and worshiping with her servants, she noticed two men walking in her direction. From the brightness of their faces and the confidence in their steps, Lydia sensed these two strangers were bringing good news. The smaller of the two men walked directly over to Lydia and introduced himself as Paul. His companion's name was Silas. All morning the two men stood by the riverside sharing the gospel of Jesus Christ. Before the day was done, the group of women confessed their faith in Jesus Christ and were baptized in the quiet waters at the river's edge.

For the first time in her life, Lydia felt alive and fulfilled in ways that she had never imagined possible. Everything had new meaning and purpose. Now she understood why the Lord had given her a thriving business and a house that was much too large for one woman and her servants to enjoy.

"Stay at my home," Lydia pleaded with Paul and Silas. "I have more than enough room. We can even have church in my courtyard and invite people from the surrounding towns."

Paul and Silas smiled at the excited woman and graciously accepted her invitation.

Lydia had dedicated herself to building a thriving business, and she gave even more of herself to building a fruitful church. When joyful Christian believers gathered in her home to hear the word of the Lord, she was fulfilled. Her glow made people love to be near her. Her kindness and hospitality knew no bounds. She gave willingly for the sake of the ministry.

One Sunday morning a Christian friend invited a dignified merchant to worship with him and his family at Lydia's house. The merchant's heart leaped as he laid eyes on this godly woman whose hands were raised to heaven, giving thanks to the Lord. Week after week the man returned to Lydia's house watching with great admiration as she expressed her deep and quiet love for God and his people. She did not seem lonely or dissatisfied with her life. She was filled with a joy that could never come from a human source.

Eventually they sat together in her garden, talking and laughing like school children. Their friendship blossomed.

One night in the quiet of his room, the merchant prayed, "Lord, I know that Lydia is completely satisfied with your love and affection. But if it's your will, let me share with her the joy that you have given us both through your Son, Jesus Christ. Give me a sign, Lord, that together we can better serve you and love you with all of our heart, all of our soul, and all of our mind."

❦

God's gifts of increase and fruitfulness are not bestowed on a few select people. Each of us can experience fruitfulness when we understand the principles of God.

The apostle John wrote these words: "To the beloved Gaius, whom I love in truth: Beloved, I pray that you may prosper in all things and be in health, just as your soul prospers" (3 John 1-2). Many believe this popular passage was a blessing pronounced over all Christians. But if you read further, through verse 8, you will see that this passage is a prayer pronounced over one person, Gaius. He was well known for his generosity and hospitality. The report had come back to John that even though Gaius was very successful, he opened his doors to help both strangers and members of the church. He gave his all for the cause of Christ.

The examples of Lydia and Gaius, whose story I imagined from what little is revealed in Acts 16, provide keys to becoming fruitful:

Have a dream. "Your old men will dream dreams, your young men will see visions" (Joel 2:28, NIV). In order to experience increase and fruitfulness in your life, you must first have a dream that reveals God's plan for your life and a vision of how to go about making your dream a reality. Dreams stir up hope and allow us to see beyond the horizon of the here and now. Three principles must be applied if you hope to make your dreams a reality:

1. *Hard work.* "I will show you my faith by my works" (James 2:18).
2. *Diligence.* "Consider [the ant's] ways and be wise, which, having no captain, overseer or ruler, provides her supplies in the summer, and gathers her food in the harvest" (Proverbs 6:6-8).
3. *Sacrifice.* "Present your bodies a living sacrifice, holy, acceptable to God, which is your reasonable service" (Romans 12:1).

Have a giving heart. "Command them to do good, to be rich in good deeds, and to be generous and willing to share" (1 Timothy 6:18, NIV). One of the great principles of fruitfulness is found in this passage. Not only does the Lord want us to give, he wants us to delight in giving, just as the Lord delights in giving us increase in every area of our lives. Even if you work hard and are fortunate enough to experience material increase, you will be miserable and suspicious of everyone you meet if you don't have a giving heart. Fruitfulness is not only about material increase. It is the increase of joy and contentment in life. No matter how much "stuff" you have, without a giving heart you are poor and needy.

Have patience. "Patient endurance is what you need now, so you will continue to do God's will. Then you will receive all that he has promised" (Hebrews 10:36, NLT). Sometimes the dreams revealed to us seem to be just around the corner. It's easy to become discouraged when months and years pass without your dream becoming a reality. But that doesn't necessarily mean you are doing something wrong or that you don't have what it takes to experience increase in your life. It may mean that you must wait for God's perfect timing and even go through a process that will prepare you for God's richest blessings. Patience is the mark of stability. It is the attribute you need in order to continue to wait without becoming discouraged. Patience produces strong character, as so many of the heroes of Scripture prove: "God made a promise to Abraham...saying, 'Surely blessing I will bless you, and multiplying I will multiply you.' And so, after he had patiently endured, he obtained the promise" (Hebrews 6:13-15).

It may sound strange to you, but my talent, my gift, and my joy in life is cleaning. That's right! I love to clean houses. My dream was to one day have my own cleaning business. And once you start talking about a dream, please know this: Words spoken out loud can bring a dream to life. And that's my story.

It all started at Ellen Goldberg's house. Even though I was a maid and she was a Jewish woman married to a successful businessman, we were the best of friends. I never dreamed that one day we would become business partners. But one morning while I was cleaning her kitchen, we started talking.

"Fatima, I don't know what you put in that bucket of yours," she said, "but when you finish cleaning my kitchen, it always smells like a forest on a spring day."

"It is a forest," I laughed. "You know those long prayer walks that I like to take in the woods? I bring back pine sap, wild sage…well, I won't go into all the ingredients."

"Whatever it is, you should bottle it and sell it!" Ellen said.

"Maybe I will!" I said, wiping off the countertops. Then with one casual slip of the tongue, I put into motion what could never be undone.

"You know, Ellen, I've been praying that one of these days the Lord would let me get enough money to start my own cleaning business. I'm going to have a van that reads: FATIMA'S CLEANING SERVICE."

Ellen placed both hands firmly on her slender waist. "Listen, sweetie, your prayers have just been answered. You have a dream and I have the money. So why not do it now?"

At first I thought I was still dreaming, but I knew it was real when Ellen helped me buy a van and wrote a big check for my supplies. In a few months my cleaning schedule was full. I didn't have to look for customers. Instead they were looking for me.

"I knew you could do it." Ellen smiled. "You're becoming a local legend with all your secret cleaning concoctions."

Things started to get so busy I decided to hire my two cousins, Patty and Aretha. Both of them were out of work, so they were real happy when I offered them jobs.

"Now you know better than that!" my mother warned when I told her I had hired my two cousins. "You three have been squabbling and fighting since you were little girls."

Fool that I am, I went against my mother's advice. By the end of the first year, I managed to pay off my loan from Ellen Goldberg. But the more money I made, the more challenges I faced with Patty and Aretha.

One morning while we were cleaning the second floor of a wealthy businessman's house, they decided to try to estimate how much money I was *really* making.

"I'm asking for a raise!" Patty said to Aretha. She threw down her dust rag and came into the bathroom where I was leaning over the bathtub scrubbing the tile. I could almost hear the crowd roaring and the bell going off to announce the start of round one of the big fight.

"Aretha and I feel like we're doing all the work and you're making all the money. So we want a raise!" Patty stood over me with her hands on both hips.

I stopped scrubbing and dropped my brush into my bucket. "Do you know how much it's costing me for insurance, cleaning supplies, advertising, and gas for the van?"

Patty rolled her eyes and sucked her teeth. "Like I said, Aretha and I want a raise!"

I was more hurt than angry. Patty was driving a new car, and Aretha was finally making enough money to get her broken-down house remodeled.

"A raise? Neither one of you could even find a job last year. That's why I hired you in the first place!" I snapped.

"We did you a favor by taking this job!" Aretha stormed into the bathroom, her nostrils flaring with anger. "We never dreamed our own cousin would treat us like slaves."

Before I knew it, I lost my temper and was about to give Aretha a free dental job. I was looking for something to hit her with when we were suddenly interrupted.

"What's going on in here?" The owner of the house stuck his head in the door where the three of us were gritting our teeth and breathing hard.

My face turned hot with embarrassment. "It's just a little misunderstanding."

"Yeah, that's all it was—a misunderstanding…but we worked it out." Aretha gave the man a phony grin.

The next day Patty and Aretha went on strike. I ended up cleaning houses day and night, trying to make up for their absence. Things finally came to a head one unforgettable afternoon as I was driving to my fourth job of the day. I didn't see the red light. I didn't see the blue Honda. I heard a crash then felt a sharp pain in my left leg. Cleaning fluids, buckets, mops, and vacuum cleaners were strewn out in the middle of the street. I was praying hard that my insurance was paid up.

"My van!" I yelled as the paramedic pulled me from the wreckage.

"Lady, you should be thankful to be alive!"

When I woke up the next morning, I was in the hospital. I wasn't the least bit surprised to see Patty and Aretha sitting by my bed with tears in their eyes.

"This is all our fault. Can you ever forgive us?" Patty whined.

Before I had a chance to get upset, the Lord filled my mind with a marvelous new idea. All this time I had been breaking my back cleaning houses when the real treasure was in my cleaning products. By the time Ellen showed up at the hospital, I was anxious to tell her about my new plans. By now you should know what happens when Ellen gets involved. The two of us perfected my line of cleaning products, and after a few years of hard work we sold the company for millions.

The other day a reporter from one of those money magazines came to see me. The two of us sat by my swimming pool talking while my maid served us lunch.

"So whatever happened to your cousins, Patty and Aretha?" she asked after I finished my story.

"They're still in the cleaning business and doing pretty well, with the help of my cleaning products," I replied with a smile.

"So what's your motto for success?" the reporter asked as she concluded her interview.

"Live a clean life and never stop dreaming," I laughed.

Though your beginning was small,
Yet your latter end would increase abundantly.

JOB 8:7

Chapter 12

The Beauty of Agate

A Woman Who Forgives and Forgets

But one thing I do: Forgetting what is behind and straining
toward what is ahead, I press on toward the goal to win the prize
for which God has called me heavenward in Christ Jesus.

PHILIPPIANS 3:13-14, NIV

The eighth jewel mounted on Aaron's breastplate, agate, was inscribed with the name of Manasseh, the oldest son of Joseph. He was born in the land of Egypt where his father rose from a common slave to governor of the land. Through the process of adoption, Manasseh became one of the twelve tribes of Israel and replaced Levi, the third son of Jacob. This was partly due to the fact that the tribe of Levi was set apart for the priesthood (see Joshua 18:7).

The name Manasseh means "forgetfulness." As noted in the previous chapter, Manasseh's father, Joseph, was sold into slavery by his brothers and later falsely imprisoned. Joseph had every right to be bitter and resentful of the people who hurt him, but something miraculous happened in his life. The Lord healed him from hurt and bitterness and allowed him to prosper and rise to power in the land of Egypt. Listen to what the Bible says about his painful past: "Joseph named his firstborn Manasseh and said, 'It is because God has made me forget all my trouble and all my father's household'" (Genesis 41:51, NIV).

Each of us was created with a God-given purpose for our time on this earth. The mission of the Lord is to cause us to forget the hindrances of the past and focus on his faithfulness as we move forward to accomplish the tasks that we were created to achieve. The mission of Satan is to cause us to forget the Lord's faithfulness and focus instead on the fears that paralyze us and keep us from embracing the purpose for which we were created.

The battle to forget the things that block our progress and focus on the Lord's plans for our lives will last a lifetime. The enemy will continue do all in his power to make us forget the goodness of the Lord.

In the Greek language the word that defines forgetfulness is *lethe*. According to Greek mythology, the Lethe River, also called the River of Forgetfulness, flowed through the realm of the underworld, where departed souls dwelled. Each soul was called upon to drink from this river, and with just one taste of this magical water, the past life on earth was completely forgotten. When people were reborn into another life, they would have no memory of a previous existence. In this place of forgetfulness, a person was free to embrace a completely new beginning.

Wouldn't it be wonderful if we could drink from a river and completely forget our old nature, which is often shaped by hurts and disappointments? The Lethe River is only a myth, of course, but life in Christ is a wonderful reality. The living waters that flow from the throne of God cause us to forget the pain of the past and move on to a glorious future with the Lord.

Prayer also can provide healing from the past as it propels us forward in our life's mission. The great mystery of prayer is that it not only allows communication with God, but it also regulates our thinking and helps us focus on the positive and productive. During the process of prayer and meditating on the Word of God, our fears are forgotten, and the faithfulness of the Lord is remembered.

Just as God removes our past to reveal our beauty, a lapidary must carefully cut and polish the agate stone to release its hidden splendor. The removal of overlying areas of stone causes this jewel to glow with shades of deep gold, orange, and pewter. The beauty of the agate reminds us not only to let go of the hurts and failures of the past, but also to let go of previous victories so that we can move on to future accomplishments. The real enemy of a successful future is trying to hold on to the glory days of your past.

The Black woman with the agate personality quickly forgets what is behind and enthusiastically presses toward new goals. She will always be found on the cutting edge of new ideas and movements. She refuses to be satisfied with her past achievements and refuses to be hindered by her past failures. Poet and author Dr. Maya Angelou wrote volumes of poetry and the best-selling book *I Know Why the Caged Bird Sings,* which was later turned into a movie of the week. But Maya Angelou did not rest on her past accomplishments. She went on to even greater achievements, among them becoming the second American poet to render an original work at a presidential inauguration. Even though she is well into her seventies, Dr. Angelou still travels, teaches, and writes.

Unlike other precious gems that are crafted into fine jewelry, the agate has many practical uses. The stones are often carved into cameos or ornate bowls and vases designed to hold precious things.

Like the agate jewel, the agate woman is as practical as she is beautiful. Her boundless energy and unbreakable spirit bring a special blessing to the man in her life. She refuses to hinder her relationship by dwelling on past mistakes and failures. Her husband will soon discover that his agate queen of African ancestry is both a giver and a forgiver. Not only does the Lord give her the strength to forgive those who have inflicted wounds, he gives her the additional strength to disregard the ungodly counsel of those who criticize her actions.

A weak woman may forgive because she feels she has no real value and therefore has no right to protest. But when family and friends accuse her of being weak and foolish, she is no longer forgiving and becomes angry again. The one who has been forgiven and thinks the matter has been settled is in for a big surprise when hit with a new wave of hostility.

True forgiveness does not come from weakness. Jesus was not weak when he hung on the cross and said, "Father, forgive them, for they do not know what they are doing" (Luke 23:34, NIV). The Bible clearly tells us that he did not hesitate to assert his authority when necessary. He rebuked the Pharisees, cast out demons, and drove the money-changers out of the temple. Every action he took, including his suffering and death, was part of a perfect plan that had been formulated to bring redemption and the Father's forgiveness to a lost and dying world.

Rahab held her newborn son in her arms as her proud husband, Salmon, stood close by, studying the child and trying to think of a name. "Let's call him Boaz. For one day he will be a man of great strength." He smiled at his wife.

Little Boaz clenched his fist and grunted loudly as his mother nodded her approval. Tears filled her eyes as her thoughts drifted back to her long-forgotten life in the city of Jericho. Indeed, the Lord had performed a miracle to bring her to this joyful day.

Rahab had been a desperate young woman who depended on the

favors of men for her survival. The unforgettable night when the Lord changed her life forever seemed at first to be no different from a hundred others. She had managed one last smile as she guided a drunken soldier to the stairs just outside her well-known establishment. She said good-bye, then closed the door behind her with a sigh of relief.

Her weary body ached as she sat down at the table, lit a lamp, and began to count the money she had made from a long day of hard work. As always the proceeds were good, but the exhausted innkeeper bowed her head and prayed to a God she didn't really know.

"God, I know you're not pleased with my life. Help me find a way out of this confusion," she whispered.

Supplying men with wine and women weighed heavy on her soul, but there seemed to be no other way to keep a roof over her family's head and food on their table. Her father was too sick to work, and her mother and younger brothers and sisters did their best to make ends meet by growing vegetables and selling baskets in the marketplace. But the officials of Jericho were wicked men who favored the rich and oppressed the poor. They levied such heavy taxes against the working class that even those who were able to find work had barely enough left over to buy food for their families.

While Rahab was still very young, an opportunity had come her way to keep her family from being sold into slavery when they were not able to pay their debts. As she stood before the magistrate to plead her father's case concerning his creditors, an older city official was taken with her beauty. The matter was quietly settled, and Rahab developed a friendship with her new benefactor. He gave her the money to open a small inn that catered to the pleasures of soldiers and wealthy landowners. As time passed, her establishment thrived. But Rahab secretly despised the greed and arrogance of her affluent patrons, especially their hatred of the poor and their open disrespect for women.

She endured their conversations about the tricks and schemes that brought them wealth and power. She showed no emotion as they laughed at the downtrodden. The men who came to her house drank strong wine while they invented new laws that were even more oppressive.

"One day God will judge every one of you," Rahab said in her heart as she refilled their cups again and again.

The weary young woman finally extinguished her lamp and went to bed. She had no idea that this would be the night that the Lord would answer her prayers and change her life forever. Just as she closed her eyes and drifted into sleep, a loud knock sounded on the door. Startled by the noise, she sat up in her bed, thinking that perhaps a group of soldiers had come to town and made their way to her inn.

"Come back tomorrow. We're closed for the night!" she shouted from the upstairs window. To her dismay, the heavy knocking grew louder and more forceful. When the mysterious visitors refused to go away, Rahab went downstairs and unlocked the front door. Fear gripped her as two men hurried inside with their swords drawn.

"Are you alone?" one of them asked as the second man searched the rooms.

"Yes, I'm alone. Who are you and what do you want?" Rahab was trembling.

"We are Israelites who mean you no harm," the taller of the two men answered as he put his sword away.

Rahab found no comfort in his words. She had heard stories of the Israelites and their great God, Jehovah. These people had defeated the Egyptians and miraculously crossed the Red Sea on dry land. The army of Israel had destroyed the Canaanites, the Amorites, and even the Midianites. Now what the people of Jericho feared the most was coming to pass. The Israelites would destroy their city.

"How can you say I have nothing to fear? If you are Israelites, you have come to make war against Jericho."

"God has judged this city and found your people guilty of many transgressions. We are nothing more than his instruments of justice."

"But what about the innocent?" Rahab pleaded. "And what about those who are sorry for their sins and seek forgiveness?"

The tall stranger stared at Rahab. For a moment she thought she saw mercy in his eyes, but she wasn't certain. "My name is Salmon; I am a spy from the army of Israel. If you give us protection and help us fulfill the purpose of the Lord, I promise to protect you from the wrath that will come."

"But what about my family? Will you also protect them?"

Salmon looked past Rahab and carefully studied the house. In spite of the elegant furnishings and artifacts collected from far off lands, her inn was evidently a place of wickedness. He rested his hand on his sword as he answered.

"Today this house is a place of sin and darkness, but soon it will become a place of light and salvation. When the army of Israel comes to destroy this city, I vow to you that all who are in this house will be saved."

With new hope and peace in her heart, Rahab helped the two men escape. On the day the city was destroyed, Rahab and her family members huddled together like frightened children as Jericho's wall collapsed around them.

"We're all going to die!" someone cried out. But when the terrible earthquake stopped, their house was still standing. Rahab was still on her knees praying to the God of Israel when Salmon and a regiment of soldiers opened her door. Rahab ran to him. When the battle was over, Rahab and Salmon stood before Joshua as her family looked on. It was declared before the assembly that all the people of Israel would honor Rahab and that her past life in Jericho would forever be forgiven and forgotten.

As Rahab gazed gratefully into the eyes of her newborn son, she could not yet realize the immensity of God's miraculous answer to her prayers. Not only did the Lord turn Rahab's shame into glory, he would honor her centuries later by allowing her to be included in the family lineage of the Lord Jesus Christ.

As Rahab's story in Joshua 2 and 6 shows, God uses cataclysmic events to shape beautiful jewels.

Eons ago, streams of hot lava flowed over valleys, rivers, and forests, locking everything that it touched in a fossilized time capsule of agate rock. The Agate Fossil Beds National Monument in Nebraska displays prehistoric animals and artifacts of every kind buried in the agate fossil beds. It's a place where those who choose to explore the past can do so to better understand the present.

In the same manner, the mind can be a place where memories remain buried for years. Buried trauma can cause lasting physical and psychological damage. As a young child I experienced the pain of being molested. Frightened and confused, I was afraid to tell my mother what had happened, but the secret trauma found a way to express itself. By the time I was ten years old, I had developed the type of stomach ulcer normally found only in adults. For years I suffered from digestive problems until I finally was able to tell my mother the terrible truth.

I have ministered to countless women who have developed illness, mood swings, or self-destructive behavior as a result of deep-seated anger and hurt. Bondage to unpleasant memories can be expressed in a wide variety of ways.

A few years ago a lovely sister came to me asking for prayer. She was suffering from a serious case of heart disease, and in spite of treatment by several specialists and extensive medical treatment she was not getting any better. As we talked about her condition, I played a game of "connect the dots" with her, where we connect a physical and emotional condition to a traumatic experience. It didn't take long to discover that the onset of her heart disease came only a few months after losing her job as a high-profile executive and going through a traumatic divorce. The healing began when this wounded sister made a commitment to forgive her ex-husband and the people at her former place of employment. In the months that followed, her heart condition began to improve.

The Lord digs up memories to release and heal us from the damaging effects of painful experiences. He often causes us to forget the pain but retain the memory so we will have a testimony to others of God's grace and goodness. Many of our worst experiences become shared wisdom once we are healed of the pain.

Forgiveness is the only real cure for the damaging effects of hurt and anger. If you are angry with God for things that have happened in your life, know that pain is a part of the process that brings about your perfection. Let go of your anger toward the Lord.

King David the psalmist suffered many things, but at some point he realized that the events of his life—all the failures and all the victories—were a part of God's divine plan. "The LORD will fulfill his purpose for me; your love, O LORD endures forever" (Psalm 138:8, NIV).

The same God who ordered David's life stands ready to help you achieve your purpose by embracing forgiveness in every area of your life:

- Forgive yourself for the mistakes of the past. Without mistakes there can be no real growth.

- Forgive those who disappointed you. Disappointments cause you to look to the Lord as your source.
- Forgive those who verbally abused you or said negative things about you. The experience will help you to be more careful with your own words.
- Forgive those who put you down or belittled you. Pray that the Lord will heal them of their own insecurities.
- Forgive those who abandoned or rejected you. Rejection is God's way of protecting you from wrong influences.
- Forgive those who betrayed you or lied to you. Betrayal builds your discernment and makes you a better judge of character.
- Forgive those who try to control or manipulate you. You will learn how to become less people-dependent and more God-dependent.
- Forgive friends and family members who have hurt you in the past. There are no perfect friends or families.

Once you complete the process of forgiveness, do yourself a big favor and erase the blackboard of your mind. You especially need to forget the things that will hinder your progress in life.

- Forget about your race and gender.
- Forget about your age.
- Forget about your background.
- Forget about your finances.
- Forget about your enemies.
- Forget about any rules but God's.
- Forget about the risks.
- Forget about your fears.
- Forget about your past failures.
- Forget about your past disappointments.

- Forget about your handicaps.
- Forget about the competition.

Second Corinthians 5:17 says, "Therefore, if anyone is in Christ, he is a new creation; the old has gone, the new has come!" (NIV). Even though Scripture assures us that in Christ we are new creations, we must still go through the process of being transformed. My dear friend Claudette Copeland once said, "Everybody wants to be transformed, but nobody wants to go through the transformation."

The process of becoming a new creation in Christ demands that we forget and forgive. It is not an easy path, but it is the best path. When the Lord is taking you through a period of transformation, look for an agate woman to help you make the journey. This sister is not hard to find. She is the one with the radiant glow of a woman who has "been there and done that."

If you're not ready to forgive and forget, she won't waste her time standing by while you have a pity party. But if you're ready to be free, she is the conductor of the Underground Railroad that will help you find a better life. The Lord uses her to help her sisters though the loss of a loved one and even a painful divorce or breakup. She is also there with wise counsel when you are promoted to a place of greater responsibility. She's the one who will whisper in your ear, "It doesn't matter if they don't like you. Just make sure you earn their respect."

The agate woman is a precious gift who should be cherished by all who are blessed with her love and friendship.

Jena walked into the Greyhound Bus station and handed the woman at the cashier's window a voucher to pay for the ticket that would get her home. After a year in a halfway house, she was finally ready to make a fresh start.

When she called home, Jena heard in her mother's voice reservations about her readiness to come home. Her older sister Jamilla refused to pick up the phone when Jena asked if she could say hello. Her sister had recently earned her master's degree in psychology, and Jena found it ironic that the new family therapist was unwilling to even speak to her.

"Welcome to reality TV," Jena said to herself as she hung up the telephone and waited to board the bus. For a moment she debated whether she really wanted to return to the drama of living with her mother, the control freak.

Jena was famous for changing her mind at the drop of a hat. But a year after giving her heart to the Lord and participating in what she called "hardcore" Bible studies, she was beginning to understand the nature of her unpredictability. At the slightest threat of danger or rejection, she was ready to jet. She had run away from an Olympic training camp when she was a highly competitive gymnast. She had run away from college when she couldn't focus on the work. And she had run away from her boyfriend when he tried to get her to face her problems.

After she ran into the cops one day as she was leaving a crackhouse, her running days ended in a jail cell.

Jena purchased a hot dog and a Sprite from the snack bar and walked back to her seat to think about her future. Suddenly it hit her: "I'm not ready for this!" Jena picked up her bag and decided to head back to the group home. She froze in her tracks as she reached the exit.

"You know what this is about," she was talking out loud to herself. "You're running again, and if you go back to the house, that's exactly what the crew is going to confront you with."

Jena took a deep breath and returned to her seat. "You know the drill—get busy!" She closed her eyes and did her memory work from Psalm 27. *"The Lord is my light and my salvation; whom shall I fear?..."* By the time Jena had recited the entire passage, she was beginning to calm down. She took out her tattered diary and a ballpoint pen and began to turn ordinary words into an art form. "Write it down and get the fear out," she whispered as her pen began to move across the page.

> Today is the first day of my freedom. I am excited, but at the same time I am afraid. I have been locked away in a prison of hatred for longer than I realized. I have surrounded myself with people who have become comfortable with their discomfort. They cannot touch, love, laugh, or share secrets because they have chosen to lock themselves away in a place where there is no forgiveness. But today the Lord has rescued me. I am forgiven and free to walk in the light of his love.

A loudspeaker announcement interrupted her flow of writing: "All aboard for Philadelphia." She closed her diary, stuck it in a side compartment of her bag, and boarded the waiting bus. Jena looked down at her watch. *Three hours to get my head together,* she thought. *Can't go back and scared to go forward... I'm not ready. I need more time.*

Her mind went back to the group home, and she envisioned herself on the hot seat, being confronted by her peers. "You need more time?! What kind of excuse is that? You had six months in prison to figure things out...so what's the real deal? Do you believe God—or were you faking it?"

Jena knows she has to answer truthfully. "My relationship with God has never been put to the test. It works in here, but what if I get out there and fail?"

A sister replies, "If you don't move on, you've already failed."

Tears welled in Jena's eyes as she watched the telephone poles pass by her window. Two hours later when the bus pulled into the rest stop, Jena dug around in her pocket for some change to call home. She needed to let her mom know what time the bus would be arriving. She needed to know how things would be when she returned home. Would her mom be cool and say, "I'll be parked outside. Look for my car"? Or would she be uptight and controlling? "Get your bags and stand directly under the Trailway sign by the Broad Street entrance. If you can't find me, call the house and leave a message, so I'll know where to locate you, blah, blah, blah."

Jena decided not to call. The thought was too scary. She might start running again, and she had just persuaded herself to see this thing through. She climbed back on the bus and began to write down how she imagined things would be:

My family is nervous. I am nervous. I'm praying on the inside, but I don't know if it's working. We try to act as though nothing ever happened. We talk about small things and hide from the big things...the big hurts and the big disappointments. We relax our bodies and try not to think about the lies and betrayals, like when Mom told my coach I was using drugs and got me kicked off the team or when I stole her money and lied about it.

"Do you want some more pie?" she asks. "Sure," I answer. She passes me the plate and I take a bite. "It's good." I smile. This is our way of touching, because we cannot come any closer right now. "Forgiveness is a process"—that's what I learned in Bible study. "Little by little, day by day. The medicines of time and God's love slowly heal the wound."

I don't know if my family has that kind of love. I don't know if I really have that kind of love. "How can we make things better?" I ask.

My mother thinks for a long time. "Well, you could help me out around the house…"

"Wrong answer" registers in her eyes.

"Oh, I know, we could go to the bookstore and sit in the coffee shop and read." This time she's on target.

"Yeah. We could read the same book and talk about it." I fight back the tears because I want to touch her hand, but I'm afraid she'll pull away. Now I know that I'm free but she's not. So I will pray for her until she's ready to forgive.

"Philadelphia, next stop!"

Jena's heart was pounding as she stepped off the bus. "Over here!" It was her sister Jamilla, waving at her with a big smile on her face.

"Sorry I couldn't talk on the phone when you called. I had some perm in my hair… I'm so broke I can't afford to go to the hairdresser—blah, blah, blah."

Jena was so happy to feel her sister's arm around her shoulder that she didn't try to hide the tears of joy that were falling from her eyes.

"Mom was busy fixing a big meal for you—all your favorite foods… you know the deal. That's why I came to get you. Besides, I really wanted to have you to myself for a little while. I'm not supposed to tell you this— Mom wanted to surprise you—but your old coach called and wants to talk to you about maybe working out with his new group of gymnasts. There might be a chance you can get back on the team."

Jena was speechless. She stared at her sister in disbelief.

"Everything's going to work out little sister," Jamilla smiled. "Let's go home!"

Blessed is he whose transgressions are forgiven,
whose sins are covered.

PSALM 32:1, NIV

Chapter 13

The Beauty of Amethyst

A Woman Who Is Trustworthy and Sober-Minded

But let us who are of the day be sober, putting on the breastplate
of faith and love, and as a helmet the hope of salvation.

1 THESSALONIANS 5:8

The amethyst was the ninth jewel mounted on Aaron's breastplate. The letters inscribed on the stone spelled out the name Benjamin, the youngest son of Jacob and Rachel and the brother of Joseph.

Rachel's life reveals a profound lesson concerning the power of the tongue. She was in great distress because her sister Leah had given birth to four sons while she remained barren. Rachel said to her husband, "Give me children, or I'll die!" (Genesis 30:1, NIV). Her words became the omen of her destruction: Rachel died shortly after giving birth to her second son, whom she called Ben-Oni, which means "son of sorrow."

Jacob later renamed him Ben-jamin, which means "son of my right hand" (see Genesis 35:18). After Joseph's brothers sold him into slavery, Benjamin became his father's favorite, his right-hand man. In Hebrew culture, the right hand is the place of dignity and honor. In a royal court the king sat his friends at his right hand because they were thought to be trustworthy. His enemies sat at his left. The Bible tells us that Jesus is seated at the right hand of God, the place of honor and power (see Hebrews 12:2).

As the son of his father's right hand, Benjamin would have been sober and trustworthy, and the royal purple of amethyst would be a fitting symbol of his attributes. *Amethyst* comes from a Greek word that means "sober." To be sober is to be well balanced, self-controlled, and trustworthy. Legend has it that when the Greeks had too much intoxicating drink, they touched the purple amethyst jewel to sober up.

A sober and trustworthy woman is a precious jewel indeed. The amethyst lady would rather talk about positive ideas than gossip. She encourages you with her words, writes a check, shows up, and helps clean up after everybody else goes home. She keeps your secrets, defends your name, and lovingly tells you the truth about yourself, even when it hurts. When other women turn their backs, she remains. When other women quit, she continues. When other women fall apart, she stands firm. When other women complain, she prays. The character of the amethyst woman has a sobering effect. Her wise judgment and godly counsel discourage foolishness.

If the Lord has blessed you with a sober and trustworthy sister-friend, please be sure to treasure her the way you would a beautiful amethyst jewel. Her loyalty is like a setting of pure gold that adds richness to her personality.

Women of African ancestry who have a sober mind-set are often told to loosen up and have some fun. Never allow anyone to convince you that you have to be a "fly girl" to be acceptable and "in the mix." The same ones who criticize you will call in the middle of the night to beg you to come to their rescue. Sober does not mean boring. You should pray and play—just don't overdo the latter.

In order to become trustworthy you must first demonstrate faithfulness and reliability. Before a ship can be called seaworthy, it must make several successful voyages carrying lives and cargo. Even though the ship will encounter storms along the way, it must safely reach its destination to be called seaworthy. In the same way, in order to be called trustworthy, a woman must first be entrusted with the "lives and cargo" of others. She must be tested over a period of time and be found—not perfect— trustworthy.

Nothing can sink the ship of trustworthiness faster than a malicious tongue. The book of James tells us that "no man can tame the tongue. It is a restless evil, full of deadly poison" (James 3:8, NIV). Malicious talk can trigger conflicts and wars. It can break up marriages and friendships and destroy reputations. It is not an exaggeration to say that the entire foundation of a person's trustworthiness rests on her ability to guard her tongue. When you gain a person's trust and prove over a period of time that you are not a malicious talker, you will be forever cherished and respected as a rare jewel indeed.

Paul sat down to write the last few pages of the letter that would be delivered to the church at Rome. He paused for a moment to give careful consideration to what he was about to say. Convinced within his own heart that he was making the right decision, he wrote, "I commend to you Phoebe our sister, who is a servant of the church in Cenchrea, that you may receive her in the Lord in a manner worthy of the saints, and assist her in whatever business she has need of you; for indeed she has been a helper of many and of myself also."

Paul finished writing the document, having permanently etched Phoebe's name in the chronicles of church history. *Phoebe is a rare jewel indeed,* Paul thought. She had proven to be a sober-minded woman with a kind spirit that caused her to sparkle with beauty. Paul thought back on the terrible winter he had spent in Cenchrea. When he was overtaken with a sudden illness, quiet and submissive Phoebe had stepped in to bring order and leadership to the ministry.

Phoebe stayed by his bed praying for him and feeding him a special herbal drink to break the raging fever. Whenever he awoke from his restless sleep, Phoebe was given instructions to pass along to the elders. When he was racked with pain and only able to communicate a few words at a time, Phoebe grasped his meaning.

"Do you want the meetings to continue?" she asked. Paul answered with an affirmative nod of his head.

On days when Paul was strong enough, Phoebe sent for scribes so he could dictate his messages to the churches. This great man of faith clearly had a strong ally in this intelligent, perceptive woman. The elders, however, were not too happy to be taking orders from a woman. Yet the anointing of the Holy Spirit rested so strongly on Phoebe that every man who feared God respected her authority. Some disagreed with her methods and were in conflict with her directives, but the beauty of Phoebe's godly focus and sober judgment helped her to overcome every obstacle.

Almost two years passed before Paul recovered fully enough to carry on with the work of the ministry. As he prepared to send the letter to Rome, he knew there might be resistance to his decision to send Phoebe. But the matter was settled; she was more qualified than any of the men in his service. Phoebe would deliver the letter and handle the sensitive matters that pertained to the church at Rome.

Paul placed his seal on the letter and handed it to Lucius, whose duty it was to encase the document for travel. Lucius stopped when his dark eyes fell on the document and mumbled, "Phoebe?"

"Is something wrong?" Paul asked, studying the deep lines in Lucius's brow.

"Nothing's wrong."

"Out with it! What's bothering you?" Paul demanded. "Does it trouble you that I'm sending a woman to Rome to handle the affairs of the church?"

"It's a dangerous trip. Christians are being arrested for the slightest infraction of the law." Lucius sighed deeply. "Besides, the business matters that need to be addressed in Rome are very complex."

"That is exactly why I am sending Phoebe," Paul protested. "She's an experienced traveler and highly skilled in handling church business."

"But will the church at Rome accept her? You know how some of the men feel about the women in places of authority."

Silence followed Lucius's words. He looked up to find Phoebe standing in the doorway.

Despite the tension, Phoebe, true to her name, gave Paul and Lucius a radiant smile. Paul opened his arms and welcomed her. Even Lucius dropped his defenses when Phoebe gently kissed his cheek.

Paul thought again about sending Phoebe to Rome. Her frame was small and her eyes so gentle. It was a difficult undertaking, but her spirit was powerful.

"Don't worry. God is with me," Phoebe said as she waited for Lucius to hand over the document. "I won't fail you."

"May the Lord send a host of angels to protect you on your journey," said Lucius, ashamed he had ever doubted her.

Paul laid hands on her and whispered a prayer. He and Lucius stood at the window and watched her walk away, carrying a letter to the Romans along with their hearts.

The name Phoebe means "pure" or "bright," and Black women like her shine as bright jewels indeed. Like this early Christian whose story I imagined from Paul's mention of her in Romans 16, the amethyst woman is trustworthy, dependable, and sober-minded. She is the voice of reason and a watchful eye. The amethyst woman has your back and can be fully trusted. Nothing misses her discerning gaze. She is bound by love to protect those close to her heart and to warn them if she senses they are on a wrong path.

Some consider the amethyst woman to be tough, aloof, and calculating. But nothing could be further from the truth. She is balanced with wisdom and kindness. It's her caring and warm-hearted nature that makes her so protective and watchful. The amethyst woman can be trusted with the most sensitive information. She is the one to call with a delicate matter or during a serious crisis.

The sober and trustworthy woman is not necessarily born with these wonderful attributes. Her character has developed through the process of spiritual maturity. As a woman spends time in service and submission to the Lord, she will gradually produce the fruit of the Spirit, among the sweetest of which are a sober mind and trustworthiness.

A sober woman has usually had a sobering experience, a situation where she asked God, "Why me?" God allows the "why me" experience to enable us to gain the wisdom and understanding that only come from facing and overcoming difficult situations.

In the book of 1 Peter, the author gives a threefold plan that can transform those who are unstable into women who are both sober and reliable:

1. Watch and pray. "Be sober, be vigilant; because your adversary the devil walks about like a roaring lion, seeking whom he may devour" (1 Peter 5:8). Before we have a sobering experience, there are usually many warning signs that are intended to force us to face reality. The amethyst woman got her learning from the school of hard knocks. Our mothers and grandmothers helped us develop sober judgment by setting us straight. I remember my mother, Barbara Louise Prunty, standing at the stove frying chicken while she listened to some crazy scheme I had come up with. Still watching over her hot skillet, she spoke her words of wisdom: "You better watch and pray!"

If you are a Spirit-filled Christian, you are linked to the voice of the Holy Spirit. The Spirit operating within you guides your decisions and warns you when you are on a wrong path. At other times, the Holy Spirit brings understanding through the Word of God. An inner voice or an uncomfortable feeling may also mark the presence of the Holy Spirit. The spiritually mature woman (which has nothing to do with age) learns to listen for the leading of God and then follows.

2. Resist the devil. "Resist [the devil], steadfast in the faith, knowing that the same sufferings are experienced by your [sisterhood] in the world" (verse 9). Picture the devil approaching you with the looks of basketball star Rick Fox, the wealth and fame of Tiger Woods, the smooth voice of Denzel Washington. The ability to resist evil even in its most alluring form is the greatest attribute of the sober-minded woman. This kind of strength comes as we pray to discern smooth lies from reality. Sadder than being deceived is a woman who deceives herself. We must abstain from even the appearance of evil. Only do things and go places where the Spirit who lives within us will be welcomed. Finally, build your spiritual muscles. Knowing we will come under attack, we build ourselves up through Bible study and prayer. Like good soldiers, we should be prepared for warfare.

3. Godliness brings spiritual growth. "But may the God of all grace, who called us to His eternal glory by Christ Jesus, after you have suffered a while, perfect, establish, strengthen, and settle you" (verse 10). Some wives are criticized by their unbelieving husbands because they serve God. Single women who live godly lives are rejected by eligible men or are passed over for job promotions because of their Christian faith. Waiting for God to move in such circumstances can be a form of suffering that perfects your patience. Standing strong in the face of rejection develops lasting character. Forgiving those who criticize you strengthens your faith. Keeping your commitment to serve the Lord, even if you suffer, will make you sober and reliable.

Scripture also gives the following insights concerning what it means to be trustworthy: "In the same way, their wives are to be women worthy of respect, not malicious talkers but temperate and trustworthy in everything" (1 Timothy 3:11, NIV). This model highlights several important aspects of becoming trustworthy:

Be a woman who is worthy of respect. In order to be trustworthy, you must first gain respect. Establish a godly standard and then do everything in your private and public life to live up to that standard. Carry yourself in a manner that precludes questions about your integrity and honor. Your speech, attire, and lifestyle all reveal that you are settled, not wild. You are known for following through on your commitments—small and great.

Be a woman who guards her words. An unruly tongue is evidence of bitterness, jealousy, or foolishness. It indicates we are not operating under the power of the Holy Spirit. I can measure my proximity to the Lord by what comes out of my mouth. A trustworthy woman also guards her tongue by keeping godly company. If you spend time around gossipers and people who disregard the well-being of others, they will eventually influence what comes out of your mouth. Again, spending time in prayer and studying the Word will safeguard you from becoming a foolish talker.

Be a woman who is temperate in all things. A temperate woman is disciplined and moderate. She knows how to have fun without going too far. She talks without talking too much. She spends money without spending too much. We all have areas where we are struggling to be temperate, such as credit-card spending or overeating. None of us is perfect, but if Jesus Christ is dwelling in our hearts and we are empowered by the Holy Spirit, our lives should reflect moderation and self-restraint.

Be a woman who guards her reputation. Sinners are watching your lifestyle to see if what you are saying about your relationship with the Lord is true. If you have been a Christian for any length of time, new Christians will look to you as an example of how to live a godly life. The Bible tells us that we are epistles read by all people (see 2 Corinthians 3:2). You may be the only example for many of what it means to be a Christian. The Lord wants unbelievers and new believers to see Christ dwelling in you.

André appeared at Carla's door with a dozen long-stem red roses and then whisked her off to a five-star restaurant. Carla smiled across the table at her handsome date. A jazz pianist played softly in the background as they shared an intimate dinner for two. Dancing at a swanky spot near the beach was on their after-dinner agenda.

Carla's heart was beating fast as she fumbled for the right words to say. André smiled as he noticed her discomfort. "What you need is something to help you relax," he said, just as the waiter appeared with two glasses and a chilled bottle of champagne.

"But I don't drink!" Carla softly protested.

"You don't have to drink. You sip champagne." He smiled and handed her a crystal glass filled with sparkling little bubbles.

"But I—"

"Please? Just one small toast to a beautiful lady and the lucky man who found her."

Carla couldn't resist his smooth words and liquid brown eyes. "Well, only a sip. I have to get up early for church in the morning." She lifted her glass.

A loud voice sounded in her head: *What do you think you're doing? Put that glass down and run for your life! Can't you see what he's up to?* Carla didn't speak, but she argued with the inner voice: *Why must you always think the worst? What am I supposed to do, ruin a beautiful evening?*

Soon the champagne was talking louder than her inner voice: *That's right, girlfriend! When's the last time a man with a good job who looked as good as André asked you out? This brother has pulled out all the stops. Relax and enjoy!*

"What's going through your pretty head?" André asked.

"I guess I'm not used to bubbly. I hope I don't oversleep and miss church in the morning." Carla giggled. Her whole body felt as light as a feather.

"Maybe you should spend the day with me tomorrow," André said. He touched her hand, and a spark of electricity traveled to her heart as he continued to play with her fingers.

"I would love to spend the day with you, but I have to sing in the choir tomorrow. Why don't you come to church with me?"

André's lips were smiling, but his eyes were frowning. "With you sitting in the choir, I wouldn't hear a thing the preacher was saying. Besides, church is not my thing."

"You do believe in God, don't you?" she asked.

"How could I not believe in God looking at a beautiful creation like you?" André lifted Carla's hand and kissed her fingers.

Carla gently pulled away. "I'm serious, André. Are you a Christian?"

André was surprised by her sober tone of voice. "Please don't tell me you're one of those holy rollers," he laughed.

"Holy...and I speak in tongues."

André crossed his arms and rested his gaze on Carla. "Well, I love a challenge. Especially, when the stakes are high and the prize is so attractive."

Carla pushed her chair away from the table. "I'm feeling a little dizzy from the champagne. Do you mind if we call it a night?"

"On one condition." André was still smiling. "If you tell me why you're so into God."

A loud thought jarred her mind: *Girl, he's running a game. Quit while you're ahead!*

A kinder inner voice interrupted: *Even if he is playing games, the Word of God doesn't come back void, so why not tell him what he wants to know?*

Carla sat on the edge of her chair trying to decide what to do. Finally, she took a deep breath and began to tell André the story about her journey with the Lord.

"I'm sorry, but we're about to close," the manager said when he came to the table hours later.

André was silent as he drove Carla back to her house. He gently put his arm around her shoulder as he walked her to her door.

"This is an evening I won't forget for a very long time." André gave Carla a warm embrace. "I would have loved to spend the evening sipping champagne, but what you shared with me was a wonderful high."

"Thank you for a lovely evening," Carla touched his handsome face before she walked inside and closed the door behind her.

Her sassy conscience was sounding a lot calmer: *Well! There could be some hope for the brother after all.*

Moments later the phone rang. It was André. "Is the invitation still open for me to go to church with you tomorrow?"

"Of course," Carla said, smiling. "I'll see you in the morning."

Be sober, be vigilant; because your adversary
the devil walks about like a roaring lion,
seeking whom he may devour.

1 Peter 5:8

Chapter 14

The Beauty of Emerald

A Woman of Rest and Good Judgment

Getting wisdom is the most important thing you can do!
And whatever else you do, get good judgment.

PROVERBS 4:7, NLT

The tenth name listed on Aaron's breastplate was that of Dan, whose name means "to judge." His name was inscribed upon a bright green emerald.

Dan was the fifth son born to Jacob. His mother was Bilhah, Rachel's handmaiden. When Jacob neared the end of his life he blessed his son Dan saying, "Dan will provide justice for his people as one of the tribes of Israel" (Genesis 49:16, NIV).

One of the most famous judges of the Bible was Samson, who descended from the tribe of Dan. Samson was as physically strong as he was morally weak. His story teaches us that before we can judge others we must first judge ourselves. When Samson chose to live continually in sexual promiscuity, the Lord judged him for his sin and allowed him to fall into the hands of his enemies. Despite Samson's moral failures, the Lord remembered his covenant with the children of Israel and let Samson regain his strength and defeat the Philistines.

The emerald in the high priest's breastplate stands as the symbol of judgment. It also serves as a reminder that we are not very different from Samson. Each of us has the potential to rebel against God's will for our lives. We want to go our own way and do our own thing. The Lord does not interfere with our free will, but he knows when our choices will lead to destruction. That's when he takes control and, as David wrote in the psalms: "He makes me lie down in green pastures, he leads me beside quiet waters, he restores my soul" (23:2-3, NIV).

When the Shepherd of our soul makes us lie down, it is always in green pastures. My late pastor, Dr. E. V. Hill, used to say that the Lord covered the whole earth with green because it's his favorite color. The beautiful emerald is the ultimate reflection of nature's glory. It is the color of springtime and summer—the time of birth and productivity. Emerald-colored plants and trees bear the fruits and vegetables that sustain us. Green represents a place of provision where all of our needs will be met.

Green is also the symbol of prosperity, rest, and revitalization. Green never tires the eyes. Perhaps this is the reason golf, with its sprawling green courses, has become such a popular pastime for overworked business and professional people looking for a relaxing sport. In Egyptian culture the emerald was worn to refresh and bring rest.

The emerald was first mined in Egypt in 3000 B.C. and gained its fame as coming from "Cleopatra's Mines." Yet the glory of Cleopatra's kingdom could never compare to emeralds described in the heavenly kingdom: "I was in the Spirit, and there before me was a throne in heaven with someone sitting on it.... A rainbow, resembling an emerald, encircled the throne" (Revelation 4:2-3, NIV). Most scholars believe the emerald rainbow surrounding the throne of God symbolizes the covenant between

God and man. The throne of God is the place of honor, authority, and judgment, and because of our sinful nature, we would be judged guilty. But mercy prevails in our lives because of the covenant sealed with the blood of Jesus Christ. The emerald rainbow is a symbol that God tempers judgment with mercy.

Just as a rainbow rejuvenates our spirits with a reminder of God's mercy, emerald women radiate a vitality that refreshes those around them. No matter what difficulties they encounter, they are like lush green trees planted by the rivers of water bringing forth fruit in their season (see Psalm 1:3). The heart of the emerald woman brings rest and rejuvenation to others. Her good judgment and godly words of encouragement are like resting in green pastures.

She has a natural gift for creating an atmosphere of rest. Her kitchen is stocked with spring water and herbal teas. Her house is filled with scented candles and comfortable furniture. She is the queen of hospitality, and she's mastered the art of keeping you company without weighing you down with idle conversation. This easygoing Black lady understands that you must have a rested mind, body, and spirit to make wise decisions and exercise good judgment.

I once was in a situation where I had only twenty-four hours to complete a very important project. I was stressed and anxious as I checked into a hotel and sat down at my computer to work. Before I started, I whispered a prayer asking the Lord to give me the strength and creativity I needed. To my surprise the Lord told me to lie down and go to sleep. I was more exhausted than I realized, because I slept for six hours. I awoke feeling upset that I had wasted most of the day, but when I started working, my thoughts were so clear that I finished the project in no time at all. I've learned that even when I'm not able to get all of the rest I need, power naps of ten to fifteen minutes can work wonders.

In my personal prayer time, I love walking in the woods and listening to the voice of God as he speaks to my heart. Green meadows and towering green trees bring rest to my spirit and inspire me to pray. No matter how difficult my life becomes, once I set my foot on emerald green pastures and smell the fresh wild sage, the cares of life grow dim.

The emerald is highly unusual because it is formed with imperfections that would diminish the value of any other jewel. A diamond with flaws would be of little commercial value. But the swirling feathers and bubbles formed inside the emerald are overlooked and even considered identifying characteristics that mark the stone as authentic and not synthetic.

The Lord sees our flaws as being like those of an emerald. They are the identifying characteristics that he uses to his glory. Peter had a fiery temper and Paul had persecuted the church, but the Lord used Peter's fiery personality and Paul's zeal to build his church.

The emerald woman lives in awareness of God's perspective. Like the scales that hang in the halls of justice, she balances her judgment with mercy because the Lord allows her to understand the nature of human flaws. She is a woman who can identify her own flaws, therefore she sees the good in people, in spite of their imperfections.

Deborah carefully filled a large bag with a sack of flour and a jug of oil and carried it to the door of her house where a hungry family anxiously waited. After she prayed, the man kissed her hand and his wife hugged her. They clutched the sack of flour, then gathered their children and hurried away. The man and his wife were hard-working farmers, but Canaanite soldiers had robbed their family of the food they had stored away.

The woman who judged Israel stood in the doorway and shook her head. She had lived long enough to remember a time when there was rest in Israel, no hunger and no enemies who oppressed them and robbed them of their grain and livestock. She had also lived long enough to see the children of Israel turn their backs on God and worship the gods of gold, silver, and sexual immorality.

Deborah noticed a dark cloud of smoke on the horizon. Once again, the Canaanites were burning and looting another village. Fear and righteous indignation engulfed her. She wondered whether the young family who had just left her house would be among the casualties of the ruthless army led by Sisera.

Deborah made her way to a clump of palm trees not far from her house. This was where she judged the children of Israel, prophesying and ministering to their needs. Deborah bowed her face to the ground and began to pray: "Lord, how long will you allow Sisera and his army to crush your people? Lord, send your deliverance."

As Deborah lay on the ground weeping and praying, the Spirit of the Lord came over her and gave her a clear vision of how Israel would be delivered.

"You want me, a woman, to organize an army?" Deborah questioned the Lord. When she lifted herself from prayer, the spirit of warfare filled her heart. She immediately called her servant. "Go get Barak and bring him to me!" she shouted.

When the young soldier finally stood before Deborah, her eyes filled with tears because she saw the anointing of the Lord resting on Barak. "The Lord has called you to gather ten thousand men of Israel and drive out the Canaanites, for he will be with you."

Barak was speechless and trembling. "I will not go unless you go with me!" he said.

Deborah issued a warning from the Lord: "If I go with you, there will be no glory in your journey, for the Lord will give Sisera into the hands of a woman."

But her words fell on deaf ears. Barak insisted that she be at his side when he went into battle. Sisera, the great Canaanite warrior, was brave and cunning, and none of the armies of the surrounding nations could subdue him. Barak did not know what to make of Deborah's prophecy. In his mind a woman could not possibly destroy this seemingly invincible man.

Barak gathered the mighty men of Israel. Deborah rode beside him into battle.

Jael, the mother of the family who had received the flour and oil from Deborah, sat quietly in her tent, praying and thanking the Lord for his faithfulness in their time of need. Now that Israel was at war with the Canaanites, times had become more difficult than ever. Wherever they went, Sisera and his brutal troops struck terror in the hearts of the people. Not only were they vandals and thieves, but they murdered innocent women and children.

Later, as she was finishing her morning chores, Jael heard someone approaching. To her surprise, a soldier walked into her tent. From his breastplate and helmet, she could tell he held a high position in the army. Little did she know that the man who stood before her was Sisera, captain of the Canaanite army.

"Do you come in peace?" Jael's voice trembled as her eyes fell on the fresh blood splattered on his clothing.

"I come in peace," Sisera replied. "I need a cool drink and a place to hide." He could hardly breathe as he stood in her tent.

Jael quietly submitted to this terrifying warrior and gave him a bowl of milk to drink. But deep inside she was enraged that this vile enemy would dare ask for her help.

The weary Sisera fell into a deep sleep, and Jael covered him with a blanket and went outside to think. "This is none of my business," she reasoned. "Soon he will wake up and be on his way, and nothing will be lost."

But as she continued to weigh the matter, the voice of wisdom and good judgment said, *What if my husband and children return early? Surely they will be dead by this soldier's hand. What if he decides to rape me or kill me so that no one will know his whereabouts? What if he leaves my house and destroys more innocent people and villages?*

In all her days Jael had never considered harming any living thing. But as Sisera slept soundly, some unseen force seemed to lead her to pick up a wooden mallet and drive a tent stake through his head.

When Barak and Deborah arrived at Jael's tent, they could hardly believe their eyes. There was Sisera, the captain of the Canaanite army, lying in a pool of blood. A frail woman stood over him, tears in her eyes.

"The judgment of the Lord has come through a woman, just as you said," Barak whispered to Deborah.

Because of Jael, rest had returned to Israel.

The natural course of good judgment is good leadership, as exemplified in Deborah's story, retold here from Judges 4. People are always drawn to those who can weigh a situation and give sound counsel. A Black woman with good judgment is bound to be a successful leader. The emerald woman is known for making prudent business and personal decisions. She has a reputation for dealing fairly with everyone. Her word is her bond, and her gift of good judgment is demonstrated in her amazing wisdom. Her restful nature and sound reasoning is a delight to the man in her life. She makes her home a refreshing sanctuary where he can relax and enjoy her company. He appreciates her as a wise counselor in whom he can trust and confide.

The Bible provides overwhelming evidence that God tempers his judgment with long-suffering, and in following his example, the emerald woman shines with patience. Discrimination and unjust laws are just a few of the problems that Black people have endured. Yet godly Black mothers, over the years, have demonstrated good judgment by helping us become better instead of bitter. In the face of unfair treatment, the emerald woman reminds us what God says about revenge: "Vengeance is Mine, I will repay," says the Lord (Romans 12:19).

Most of us have asked ourselves: Where is God's justice concerning Black families who were torn apart and deprived of education and economic opportunities by slavery and ongoing discrimination? These unfair practices remind us of several important factors about the Lord's judgment:

All judgment does not take place in the earthly realm. Those who commit injustices may appear to live a full life on earth, but one day they will stand before the judgment seat of Christ and answer for their wicked deeds. In Luke 16, we read the story of Lazarus, the beggar who was rewarded while the rich man who ignored his need went to hell. This is a perfect example of the righteous judgment of God. The ungodly will be condemned at the time of judgment. Sinners will have no place among the godly (see Psalm 1:5, TLB).

We will not always see the judgment of God against our enemies. When people commit acts of injustice, God sometimes will judge them right here on earth, though we may never see it. Abel did not live to see God's judgment against his brother Cain, but the Lord sentenced him to suffer for the rest of his life, wandering as a vagabond and a fugitive. And the Lord said to Cain, "What have you done? The voice of your brother's blood cries out to Me from the ground. So now you are cursed from the earth" (Genesis 4:10-11).

God's judgment may fall on those who sin and their families. The children are often faced with generational curses that can only be destroyed by the blood of Jesus. In 2 Samuel 11, we read that David killed a soldier named Uriah after he'd taken his wife, Bathsheba. Uriah did not live to see the Lord's judgment against David, but David and his children suffered because of his wrongdoing. "For I, the LORD your God, am a jealous God, visiting the iniquity of the fathers upon the children to the third and fourth generations of those who hate Me" (Deuteronomy 5:9).

In spite of the many injustices in this world, God is at work in the lives of Black women and their families. During slavery our foreparents were forced to work without any compensation. When slavery ended, each Black family was promised forty acres of land and a mule. As many of us know, the American government never paid its debt. Today, less than one hundred fifty years after the Emancipation Proclamation, a mysterious phenomenon makes me think that the judgment of God has ruled in favor of former slaves by compensating their descendants.

Many Black athletes and entertainers, some still in their teens and early twenties, are becoming instant millionaires. All around the world they are respected and celebrated by people of all races and creeds. For example, eighteen-year-old basketball player Lebron James signed a ninety million dollar contract with Nike.

Men and women from other races must now compete with these supertalented descendants of slaves. The proud Black mothers who once stood in welfare lines, prayed, and made sacrifices are now lifted to a place of honor by their celebrated sons and daughters. Even those who are not drafted into professional sports are receiving athletic scholarships to the best schools and gaining a quality education without their parents having to pay the costly tuition.

Perhaps we are seeing God's hand of judgment, which does not always work in the way we expect. In fact, judgment can take many forms. *Dan* is a Hebrew word that means "to execute punishment or reward." *Shafat* is a word used more frequently for "judgment." It also means "to vindicate or condemn." Judgment related to discernment and discretion is indicated by the Hebrew word *tam,* which means "to examine by tasting." In the Hebrew tradition, the metaphor of tasting in order to come to a correct decision was often used.

Psalm 34:8 says, "Oh, taste and see that the LORD is good." Since our taste buds are not connected to our vision, we know that the psalmist was not talking about food or drink when he said "taste and see." The writer is using the word *taste* as a metaphor to describe the goodness of the Lord. We must use our discerning taste to judge—whether we're judging the goodness of God or the trustworthiness of a man.

The Hebrew word *tam* helps define five characteristics of an emerald woman:

Taste. "As a ring of gold in a swine's snout, so is a lovely woman who lacks discretion" (Proverbs 11:22). A woman with good taste possesses a quiet dignity that money cannot buy. Her style of dress is fashionable yet modest. Her surroundings are clean and orderly, and her friends are sober and godly.

Discretion. "May you be blessed for your good judgment and for keeping me from bloodshed this day and from avenging myself with my own hands" (1 Samuel 25:33, NIV). The discreet woman never loses her composure when the pressure is on. She knows how to pray and then wait on the guidance of the Holy Spirit. This gracious lady can whisper a few words and a sensitive matter will be settled. She knows how to negotiate without causing conflict.

Perception. "So [Samuel] arose and went to Eli, and said, 'Here I am, for you did call me.' Then Eli perceived that the LORD had called the boy" (1 Samuel 3:8). The perceptive woman understands the deeper meaning in an action or an event. This woman, who has become perceptive through spiritual growth, is sensitive to the presence of good or evil. She is also sensitive to the deepest needs of people in her life.

Discernment. "Then Pharaoh said to Joseph, 'Inasmuch as God has shown you all this, there is no one as discerning and wise as you'" (Genesis 41:39). Because of her intimacy with the Lord, the discerning woman can detect the hidden motives of those who cloak themselves with deceptive ploys. She can judge the difference between what is real and what is pretense.

Wisdom. "Teach me good judgment and knowledge, for I believe Your commandments" (Psalm 119:66). Good judgment is a facet of wisdom bestowed upon a woman who makes an investment in seeking the knowledge of God. This, coupled with her life experience, causes her to shine like a beacon of hope for those who need spiritual guidance. People cherish her spiritual understanding and the examples she sets for godly living.

If you know a woman with these five qualities, treasure this emerald friend and listen to her carefully. Her keen judgment can lead you to a place of rest.

Princess Yaa Asantewaa looked forward to taking her morning stroll down to the river's edge, where she hoped to catch a glimpse of Kofi, a handsome young warrior. Her brother Kwame noticed the light in her eyes when she looked at Kofi and immediately warned her of the consequences of such an attachment.

"Do you want trouble to come like a swarm of bees into Kofi's life? Because that is exactly what will happen if Father suspects that there is something going on between you and a commoner. You are already pledged in marriage to a chief."

Yaa was angry and defiant as she listened to her brother's words. "I have never even spoken to Kofi," she fumed. "But if I choose to do so, you can't stop me!"

Later in the day, the princess stood by the river's edge watching Kofi with a group of young men who were beating metal into hunting spears. She made no attempt to hide her interest as she watched the beads of sweat ripple down his muscular arms. They made conversation with their eyes, not caring if anyone was watching.

A little boy came and sat next to Princess Yaa. "Go tell Kofi to meet me here by the river just as soon as the sun goes down," she ordered. The boy ran over to the group of men and whispered in Kofi's ear. The handsome warrior nodded at the princess, then returned to his work.

That night in the bright moonlight under a clump of trees, the two young lovers were alone for the first time. "I have been waiting for this moment," he said as he held her close.

"My father will never let us marry. Let's run away together and find a place to be happy," she whispered.

"Your wish is my command." Kofi kissed her gently. "We will leave tomorrow night and take the trade route north. I have friends in the city of Tumu."

That next night, as planned, Princess Yaa and Kofi left the village and headed north.

As the dawn broke across the African sky, they sat beneath a sprawling tree eating fish Kofi had caught in a nearby river. He tried to enjoy the company of his soon-to-be wife, but he felt uneasiness in the air. Perhaps men from their village had followed him and the princess. Moments later a much worse fate overtook them when White slave traders threw nets over their bodies. Kofi fought with the strength of ten men, but a blow to the head knocked him unconscious.

"Looks like we got ourselves a royal lady from the Edweso tribe. We can make a lot of money ransoming her back to the chief," one of the men commented as he studied the tribal markings on Princess Yaa's right arm.

Yaa screamed and clawed like a wild woman as two men put her in shackles and then headed for Kumasi, leaving Kofi bleeding on the ground. That was the last she saw of Kofi.

Years passed slowly after Yaa's return home, and eventually she was forced to marry a much older neighboring chief. The aging king was kind, and together they had children. After her husband's death, she became the queen mother of the region, settling disputes and making political decisions.

Deep in her heart she still longed for Kofi. For this reason she had a deep hatred for slave traders and all other White intruders. Not only did they take unfair advantage of her people, but they had separated her from the only man she ever loved.

In the autumn of her years, the British took complete control of the gold mines of the region, and the young tribal leaders led a bloody but unsuccessful rebellion. Among those who were seized and sent into exile by the British was young prince Kwasi, the grandson of Queen Yaa.

The British demanded that the Ashanti elders surrender the golden stool, the symbol of Ashanti authority. Queen Yaa resisted and called all to arms. With a regal face that resembled carved mahogany, she stood in front of the men and said, "The British are eating our lives away like an army of worms boring into freshly ripened fruit. The Ashanti land was once like a restful garden where its people lived in peace and knew days of abundance. Wars between tribes were more rare than the sighting of an ibis bird, and they were quickly settled with the exchange of goats and a few sacks of gold. But then the hungry beasts appeared on our shores, devouring everything. They are never satisfied."

The men mumbled and nodded their heads in agreement.

"When the British took my grandson from my side and slaughtered our young children, they gave me something to die for. Are you ready to die so our people might live again?"

A great chant filled the compound as the Ashanti chiefs and men of war joined forces with Queen Yaa and vowed to drive the British from their shores. In a few days the Ashanti warriors surrounded the British fort at Kumasi with queen mother Yaa Asantewaa leading the revolt. Blood would be shed and justice would finally come to the Ashanti people.*

Village life ceased, it ceased in Israel,
Until I, Deborah, arose.
Arose a mother in Israel.

JUDGES 5:7

---

* Queen Yaa Asantewaa is a historical figure. She led the Ashanti nation in
  what is now Ghana in the war of 1900 against the British. It became known
  as the Yaa Asantewaa War. Ghana still celebrates this warrior queen.

Chapter 15

The Beauty of Onyx

A Woman of Happiness and Abundance

The hopes of the godly result in happiness,
but the expectations of the wicked are all in vain.

PROVERBS 10:28, NLT

On the breastplate of Aaron, the onyx jewel was in the eleventh position. It was engraved with the name Asher.

Asher was the eighth son born to Jacob. His mother was Zilpah, the maidservant of Leah. When he was born, Leah proclaimed, "'I am happy, for the daughters will call me blessed.' So she called his name Asher" (Genesis 30:13).

The Hebrew translation for the name Asher means "happy or blessed," and this son found both happiness and abundance. When Jacob pronounced a final blessing over his sons, he said of Asher, "Bread from Asher shall be rich, and he shall yield royal dainties" (Genesis 49:20).

The Lord blessed Leah and caused her to be fruitful because she was not loved. Perhaps because of Zilpah's lowly position, the Lord elevated her son Asher above his brothers. When Moses spoke a blessing over Asher, he said: "Asher is most blessed of sons; let him be favored by his brothers" (Deuteronomy 33:24). The tribe of Asher went on to prosper as traders. They were indeed a happy and blessed people who rose to prominence and experienced great abundance.

Onyx, a variety of quartz, is a strong stone with a smooth, black shiny surface. It is solid rather than transparent and is widely used for engraving, sculpting, carving art, and jewelry. The onyx served a very important purpose in the spiritual life of Israel. Moses was directed by God to use the onyx jewel in the following manner: "Then you shall take two onyx stones and engrave on them the names of the sons of Israel: six of their names on one stone and the remaining six names on the other stone, according to their birth.... And you shall put the two stones on the shoulders of the ephod as memorial stones for the sons of Israel" (Exodus 28:9-10,12).

The ephod was a sleeveless coat worn by the high priest. The coat was fastened on each shoulder with the two engraved onyx stones, which bore the names of each tribe. Symbolically the onyx stones held the twelve tribes together and kept them connected as a family.

In every Black clan, one woman carries the members of her family like an engraved onyx jewel in her heart. This grandmother, mother, aunt, cousin, godmother, or big sister shares their hopes and dreams, their hurts and needs. She is the ambassador of peace and promotes family unity, often using reunions, barbecues, picnics, weddings, and even funerals to encourage her family to come together with love and laughter.

The Black woman who is like polished onyx doesn't require her world to be perfect to enjoy life. A happy heart is her trademark. She can start a party around her kitchen table. A wooden spoon suddenly becomes her microphone and an old cotton shift serves as an evening gown as she lip-syncs a song on the radio. This onyx woman is always reflecting on the happiness that comes from the Lord. She sees life in Christ as joyful rather than stuffy and rigid. The fun starts when she arrives. She's animated and full of laughter. She laughs at herself and helps others laugh at themselves. When she's around, everyone is given a pocketful of smiles and departs with happy memories.

For some, happiness is hard to find. Even when the burdens of oppression become less weighty and they have money to spend, many still search for happiness. Young and beautiful or older and settled, married or single, with or without children, they are desperately searching for the elusive land of happiness. So many miss the chance to be happy because they're looking for it in the wrong places.

Happiness can be likened to a bag of jewels owned by a traveler who on his journey encountered a man of questionable character. The two men shared a small room at an inn, and as night was falling, the traveler carrying the valuable jewels worried that they might be stolen while he slept. Then he came up with an idea: He hid his jewels under the pillow of the suspected thief. Once he fell asleep, his roommate did just as the traveler suspected he would. All through the night the would-be thief searched for the precious jewels, never realizing they were already in his possession.

The onyx woman has an eye for happiness and knows where to find it. She never overlooks the gifts that God has designed to bring her happiness. If you were to ask this precious Black jewel what real happiness is, she would probably answer: "Happiness is being cancer free or a cancer survivor. Happiness is living in a free country where you are free to work, raise your family, and freely worship God. Happiness is being able to help others instead of needing help. Happiness is a good cup of coffee or a good-looking man nodding as he passes by. Happiness is a snowball fight in the winter, followed by a movie and a piping-hot pizza. Happiness is a new pair of shoes that feel good on your feet. Happiness is graduation day or your team winning the championship."

Stop looking at the big picture of how you wish your life could be someday and begin now to enjoy the small snapshots of the perfect moments in life that will never come again.

Real happiness and abundance can only come from God. The Bible gives us three simple directives in Psalm 1:1 to bring happiness and abundance into our lives.

1. Do not walk in the counsel (advice) of the ungodly. Talk-show hosts, rappers, and false religious leaders lead many to places where happiness can never be found. To walk with the Lord means to be counter-cultural, to dare to be different from the world. Rebelling against God's Word leads to sin, disease, and heartbreak. Turn off the television, CD player, and radio. Find a Bible study group and a pastor to give you godly advice that can be applied to your daily life. Then you can walk in the direction that leads to true happiness and abundance.

2. Don't stand in the path (or make friends) with sinners. So much of what seems enticing—activities that take place in glamorous settings, people who wear beautiful clothes and live in awesome houses and drive fancy cars—merely produces fake thrills designed to entrap your soul. Counterfeit beauty and excitement are not happiness; they're simply a snare to pull you into sin. Sin robs us of happiness, and soon that counterfeit excitement is replaced by very real pain. Sin destroys us physically, mentally, and emotionally. But the path of the Lord leads to happiness and abundance.

3. Don't sit down with scorners. To sit denotes listening and spending time. Scorners or God-haters are those nice people, our family, friends, classmates, and coworkers with whom we get along just fine until we bring up prayer, the Bible, or Jesus. They have no love and reverence for God. They are not afraid to ridicule or defy God. If possible, stay away from such people. Pray for them if you can't get way from them. Don't let them rob you of your happiness.

If you will follow these directives, Psalm 1:3 promises a fruitful life of abundance: And you "shall be like a tree planted by the rivers of water, that brings forth its fruit in its season, whose leaf also shall not wither; and whatever [you do] shall prosper."

Ruth strolled through the marketplace with her son Obed following close behind. She gave no thought to the admiring glances of the women who whispered, "She's very wealthy. Just look at her fine linen robe and gold bracelets."

"I wish I could be like her, so beautiful with a rich husband and a fine son."

"That would make me happy," another woman sighed.

Ruth's husband, Boaz, was a wealthy man. The Lord had blessed the works of his hands; he blessed him with children, blessed his fields, and blessed his flocks. But the greatest blessing was the love that flowed like an endless bubbling spring between him and Ruth.

Boaz cherished Ruth for her grateful heart. She never took his kindness for granted and was amazed at the Lord's continuous blessings. It was not unusual for Boaz to find Ruth on her knees giving thanks to the Lord for the smallest things: "Lord, you are so good to me. You have given me a husband who showers me with kindness, and he is such a good father to our son. I thank you, Lord, for his laughter. I pray that I will always bring joy to his heart. Thank you for giving us a happy home. I praise and bless your name."

Ruth was happy with her life. Bur her one worry was that her son, Obed, would grow up and take the blessings of the Lord for granted. "Finish your food," Ruth said to him one morning at breakfast. "I know what it's like not having anything to eat. That's why I never want you to waste food."

Obed smiled at her. "Mother, why are you saying such things? You have never been poor or hungry," he laughed.

Ruth gave Obed a long look and thought of her torturous journey, years before. Under the burning sun with no food and very little water, she and her mother-in-law, Naomi, traveled from her homeland of Moab, beyond the Dead Sea, through the desert, all the way to her new home in Bethlehem—Naomi's birthplace. Robbers or wild animals could have attacked them, but the Lord kept them safe. When they finally reached their destination, a kind relative welcomed them into her house and offered the two women a cup of milk and a loaf of freshly baked bread. Nothing Ruth had eaten since had tasted quite as good.

Arriving in Bethlehem was one of the happiest times of her life; the splendor of her present surroundings could never diminish the memory of that day.

"Why are you smiling?" Obed interrupted his mother's thoughts.

"I was thinking about the day I came to this city and how happy I was. Your grandmother Naomi and I were very poor, and we had no one to take care of us. Your father was very kind. He let me work as a gleaner in his fields so your grandmother and I would have food to eat. He even told his foreman to make sure that I was given extra grain." Ruth smiled. "As time went on, your father fell in love with me, and the Lord blessed me to become his wife."

"You couldn't have been a gleaner. They are dirty, worthless people," he frowned.

"Who told you such a terrible thing?" Ruth demanded, her heart troubled.

Obed hesitated to answer. "Well, I heard one of the servants talking. He said that the gleaners were either heathens from foreign lands or bad people God was punishing for disobeying his laws."

"Dear one, that is not true. Perhaps there are some bad people among the gleaners. But there are also bad people among those who own houses and land.

"I was just a young girl when I came to Bethlehem from the land of Moab. I am from a foreign land. My father-in-law and my first husband died, and there was no one to take care of Grandmother Naomi and me. But we trusted the Lord. Terrible things can happen to women who have no one to take care of them. They often become beggars in the streets and even worse. Without your father's help, I am not sure what would have happened to us."

Obed was silent. He had never before heard about his mother's background. He had never known hungry people who had nowhere to live.

Ruth looked at Obed's smooth hands and finely made sandals and said, "Tomorrow, I want you to go to the fields and help the gleaners."

Her words shocked Obed, but in spite of his protest and with the consent of her husband, Ruth sent her son to the fields to live and work with the field hands and gleaners.

After five hot, tiring days in the fields, Obed returned to the house, bringing another young boy with him. Obed's skin was baked from the sun and the palms of his hands were callous; yet he wore a bright smile.

"My poor son, I know you are glad to be home," Ruth said with compassion.

"No, Mother! I had the best time of my life."

"And who is your friend?" Ruth asked.

"This is Nathan," Obed said, full of excitement. "I met him while I was working in the fields. His mother and father died and he has no place to live, so I brought him home to stay with us. It's okay for him to stay, isn't it, Mother?"

As the two boys sat down for dinner, Ruth had never seen her son look so happy. Nathan was smiling, too, as he ate heartily.

Abundance does not mean gathering and hoarding material things; it means being satisfied and content with what you are acquiring and achieving. It also means being in a position to be a blessing to others like the woman in this story, which was, of course, inspired by the biblical character Ruth.

As a single woman, I am not interested in living in a mansion. If someone gave me a spacious house with manicured lawns, I would probably live in one of the rooms and turn the additional space into a home for unwed mothers. Abundance for me is a hot bath, fluffy towels, and lots of fancy soaps and oils—and enough money to give regularly to help people and ministries.

What makes me content and satisfied might not work for you. You might have a growing family and love living in a big house with a sprawling lawn. The danger is in defining happiness by someone else's standards.

Many lack real abundance because they have been deceived by the greed in our culture and in their hearts. Greed is abusing yourself and misusing others for the sake of material gain. Greed is the dark side of abundance, fueled by selfishness. Greed will cause you to have more than you need, yet refuse to share.

You cannot be greedy and happy at the same time. The greedy constantly worry about their possessions. They are afraid someone will rob them or trick them out of what they own. But greed itself is the robber and trickster who will take your happiness.

Be careful. Abundance is not worth sacrificing the things that once brought you happiness and contentment.

Nothing is more unattractive than a woman who is consumed with greed and will sacrifice the well-being of others to satisfy her own appetite. A greedy wife drains a husband, but a wife who is willing to work with her husband to achieve God's plan for abundance is a blessing.

Remain prayerful and watchful that your abundance does not turn into greed. Set your own personal boundaries regarding what is "enough." If your standard of what is "enough" results in conflict with your family or causes declining health or bouts with fatigue and depression, then rethink your priorities.

Abundance and happiness come when we embrace wisdom from the Lord. Proverbs says, "Happy is the [person] who finds wisdom.... Length of days is in her right hand, in her left hand riches and honor" (3:13,16). In our quest for happiness and abundance, the goal is balance. We sometimes end up sacrificing one in order to have the other.

Proverbs 31 reveals how the onyx woman finds balance in her abundance:

"She considers a field and buys it; from her profits she plants a vineyard" (verse 16). Work hard and smart. Get involved in money-making ventures, but do not spend all of your profits. Learn how to make wise investments.

"She extends her hand to the poor, yes, she reaches out her hands to the needy" (verse 20). Luke 6:38 says to those who give that the Lord will give back to you, "good measure, pressed down, shaken together, and running over." "Running over" signifies abundance. Remember the poor, and you will always experience abundance in your life.

"Her husband is known in the gates, when he sits among the elders of the land" (verse 23). Take good care of the man who is taking care of you. As a caring partner, your tasks might include evaluating your husband's ideas. Help him with his grooming. Provide healthy meals and entertain friends.

"She opens her mouth with wisdom, and on her tongue is the law of kindness" (verse 26). Understand the power of words. Fragrant, kind words will always be rewarded. Use your words to encourage, motivate, and lovingly correct. Give knowledge and understanding and don't waste talk about things that are unprofitable.

"She watches over the ways of her household, and does not eat the bread of idleness. Her children rise up and call her blessed; her husband also, and he praises her" (verses 27-28). Don't spend time gossiping on the phone or watching television. Balance your time between work, pursuing goals, and family. Generate income (from home or office) while giving your family the love, care, and attention that only you can give.

Many Black women grew up in neighborhoods of have-nots and faced tremendous struggles to "make it." But once you make it, you sometimes find it difficult to distinguish between need and greed. Your kids have lots of stuff, but you can't spare them much of your time. You own enough shoes and clothing to open a small boutique, but you have no special man to wear them for, or you don't have time to dress up for a quiet dinner with your husband.

In Matthew 4:8-9, the devil offered Jesus all the kingdoms of the world and their glory if Jesus would bow down and worship him. Jesus responded by saying, "Away with you, Satan! For it is written, 'You shall worship the LORD your God, and Him only you shall serve'" (verse 10). Notice that Satan could only offer Jesus material things. Peace, love, and happiness belong exclusively to God.

In your efforts to find happiness and abundance, consider the times in your life when you were happy with little. My happiest memories include getting out of grade school for the summer and heading south to the small town of Oriole, Maryland. Every summer our family spent three wonderful months in a house with no plumbing and a smelly outdoor toilet. There was a lot of prejudice in the South, but it never stopped us from having fun. At the crack of dawn my brother, sisters, cousins, and I would stand on the side of the road and wait to be picked up by a truck that would take us to a farm to pick tomatoes. We got paid fifty cents a basket, and when the day was over, we were dropped off in front of the country store where we spent our hard-earned money on ice cream and cold drinks. In the evening, we sat on the front porch swatting flies and mosquitoes, and playing card games and Dominoes. On Sunday mornings we sang in the youth choir that my mother directed.

Money can't buy the precious memories of those summers I spent swimming in a muddy creek and picking tomatoes with my brother, Sonny; my sisters, Marlene and Lillian; my aunt Linda; and my cousins Mary Jane, Walter, and June Bug.

Those who love money will never have enough. How absurd to think that wealth brings true happiness! (See Ecclesiastes 5:10.)

Marilyn looked at the pile of work on her desk and then at the clock on the wall. *I need a break,* she thought, and chose to ignore the frantically ringing phone. It had been days since she had even considered taking her lunch hour. Looking from her office window at the sunny sky and the trees swaying in the breeze, she made an executive decision to pick up a sandwich from the deli across the street and walk to the nearby park.

After a refreshing stroll among children at play, Marilyn found a bench and sat down to relax. Her plain blue dress and out-of-style shoes made her feel dull and boring. Angry with herself for allowing her job to consume so much of her life, she also felt helpless about her situation. She could see no way to escape. She'd invested too many years toward retirement to quit. And that distant reward was all she could expect for the mountain of work that was constantly dropped into her lap. She had plenty of vacation time saved up but never seemed to get around to taking it. Marilyn had no love life and no cluster of friends or family to break the cycle of working, eating, sleeping, and growing older. Her body felt tight with frustration. She finished her tasteless sandwich, picked up her book, and began to read, but her eyes wouldn't focus. She stared at the pages, trying not to think about her job and her life.

Marilyn barely noticed when the laughter of children playing exploded into loud squeals of joy. The sprinkler system that watered the soft grass had suddenly come on, trapping the children in the cool showers.

Sitting just out of range of the sprinklers, Marilyn thought, *How awful. Their clothes are getting wet.* But as she watched the youngsters, soaked to the bone, singing and dancing beneath the summer sun, turning flips, racing in and out of the gushes, she realized that they were having the time of their lives. She smiled at the delightful frenzy. Suddenly the wind shifted, and Marilyn's eyes blinked as the cool water splashed against her skin. Her body felt as light as a feather.

"Hey kid! Wanna play?"

Kid? Who are they talking to? Marilyn wondered.

"We're talking to you!" came the reply. "Put the book down and come on!"

As if some strange force had taken possession of her, Marilyn ran toward the children. She didn't mind as the sprinklers sprayed her powdered face and permed hair.

"You're it!" A girl tagged Marilyn and then disappeared behind a tree. Marilyn's dress and shoes were soaked, but she didn't care at all as she chased after the girl, laughing with glee.

"I want to stay in this place forever!" she yelled at the top of her lungs as they all danced around in one big circle.

With those words everyone stopped and looked at her. One of the girls in the circle nudged a skinny boy with eyeglasses, urging him to speak.

"You can't stay here forever," the boy said.

"But why?" Marilyn felt confused.

"Because it wouldn't feel the same if you stayed here all the time. That's what makes it so much fun—'cause it's only for a little while."

Marilyn hung her head as she spoke again. "If I leave, I'll never be this happy again."

A little girl with big bright eyes looked at her. "Then why don't you take the happy thoughts with you? So whenever you feel sad, you can close your eyes and think of the cool showers, the sunshine, and the fun we had. Then you'll be happy again."

"But what if I lose the happy thoughts and can't find them?" Marilyn tried to reason with the children.

"Then find some more," the boy with the glasses laughed.

At that moment the sprinklers stopped, and the children began to say good-bye. Marilyn reluctantly bid them farewell, but as she walked back to the office, she smiled. She even found herself giggling.

"What's so funny about getting caught by the park sprinklers?" one of her coworkers asked. "Why didn't you try to get out of the way? You look a mess."

Marilyn was still smiling as she looked down at her wet clothing. "I think I'll go home and change," she announced. "Then I'm going out to play. I'll be back in a couple of weeks."

> *A merry heart does good, like medicine,*
> *But a broken spirit dries the bones.*
>
> PROVERBS 17:22

Chapter 16

The Beauty of Pearl

A Woman of Wisdom and Kindness

She opens her mouth with wisdom,
And on her tongue is the law of kindness.

PROVERBS 31:26

Naphtali, whose name means "my wrestling," is named in the twelfth position on the breastplate of Aaron. Scholars believe that perhaps it was the jasper stone that represented the tribe of Naphtali, but I think it would be more interesting to link Naphtali to the pearl. I say this because it is a wrestling match that forms the pearl. When an intruder manages to invade the oyster, the battle begins. The oyster must fight to overcome the invader.

In the ongoing struggle to produce Jacob's offspring, Rachel called on her maidservant Bilhah to bear children on her behalf. Bilhah's second son by Jacob was Naphtali, and at the birth of Naphtali Rachel said: " 'With great wrestlings I have wrestled with my sister, and indeed I have prevailed.' So she called his name Naphtali" (Genesis 30:8).

Rachel was a self-proclaimed wrestler. Even though the Lord blessed her with Naphtali, she found no peace. She continued to wrestle with her sister Leah in an attempt to win her husband's affection. She came up with one scheme after another, but they all ended in frustration. Without the wisdom of the Lord, we will always find ourselves wrestling in vain over the challenges that life will bring our way.

Naphtali's father was a wrestler as well, having fought and tricked his way into receiving the blessing meant for his firstborn brother, Esau. Jacob was a con artist, but his evil deeds caught up with him. One night when Jacob was running from his twin brother, Esau, not long after Naphtali's birth, he found himself involved in a wrestling match with God. As he wrestled with God, he declared, "I will not let You go unless You bless me!" (Genesis 32:26). That night the Lord changed Jacob's name to Israel, which means "you have struggled with God and with men, and have prevailed" (verse 28). Jacob's twelve sons became known as the twelve tribes of Israel.

After the wrestling match with God, Jacob underwent a change, like a grain of sand being transformed into a precious pearl. Sometimes, nothing short of a wrestling match with God will separate us from foolish and selfish behavior. God transformed Jacob, the heartless trickster, into Israel, a man of wisdom and kindness.

And he works the same miracle of change in any woman he designs to be a pearl. "The kingdom of heaven is like a merchant looking for fine pearls. When he found one of great value, he went away and sold everything he had and bought it" (Matthew 13:45-46, NIV).

In this parable of Jesus, the merchant took a drastic action. What set that particular pearl apart from all the others? What qualities in the pearl prompted this man—who was probably an expert on pearls—to give everything he had to possess it?

Large, perfectly shaped pearls rank among the most precious of jewels. Pearls also come in a variety of colors, including pastels. White is the most popular color, but among the most valuable is the black pearl.

The merchant in the parable probably saw a big and perfectly formed pearl. Perhaps it was a shimmering, iridescent white or the color of freshly churned cream or maybe a soft, baby pink. But because it was both rare and extremely valuable, it's not unlikely that this particular jewel was a beautiful black pearl.

Black pearls also come in the human variety. These women are known for their wisdom, kindness, and creative survival skills. From the time of slavery to the mid-1950s, Pearl was an extremely popular name among Black women, and some full-figured ladies were called "Big Pearl."

Unlike precious jewels developed in the heat and pressure of the earth, pearls are formed in troubled waters. In fact, trouble is at the core of every pearl. Oysters produce most pearls, and inside the oyster shell is a smooth, fleshy tissue that serves as a tasty seafood dish. The oyster must open itself up to take in food and to rid itself of waste. When a pebble, a grain of sand, or a parasite gets inside the shell, the oyster secretes a calcium carbonate mineral substance around the troubling intruder. Layers of the calcium substance are wrapped around it until the irritating matter inside the oyster is completely covered, forming a smooth pearl and creating a comfortable, nonirritating environment inside the shell. The bigger the problem inside the shell, the bigger and more valuable the pearl produced.

Just as oysters turn their irritations into pearls, women of African ancestry produce pearls of wisdom and pearls of greatness out of their trials. In order to survive as Black women, we must open ourselves up to forces that have the power to destroy our potential and our plans for the future. In the process of reaching for our goals, irritating encounters abound. Black women have learned how to cover pain and adversity with beautiful layers of pearl made from prayer, faith, and patience.

There is also a valuable lesson to be learned about the difference between natural pearls and cultured pearls. A natural pearl is formed when foreign particles work themselves inside the oyster's shell as described earlier. A cultured pearl is produced inside oysters that are *injected* with irritating particles. The oyster is forced to emit the pearl-producing calcium carbonate.

The wrestling match you face may be a natural part of living, or it may be a special challenge allowed by the Lord. Both have the potential to produce precious pearls of wisdom in your life. "And we know that all things work together for good to those who love God, to those who are the called according to His purpose" (Romans 8:28).

Jedida moved through the middle of the dusty vineyard, walking slowly up and down each row and pulling at the stubborn weeds that tangled themselves around the budding grapes. Her back throbbed with pain, and the heat from the sun pressed so hard against her skin that sweat fell like teardrops, drenching her face and neck. Finally, when she was so exhausted that she could not pull another weed, she straightened her aching body. The sunbaked woman made her way to a nearby stream and found a spot beneath a clump of trees that blocked out the hot sun. She lay on her face and drank deeply from the cool stream.

Jedida tried not to think about the reason that she was working in this miserable vineyard. She closed her eyes and dipped her hair into the refreshing stream, hoping to silence her thoughts. Then she stretched out on the grass to rest her tired body.

It had been a year since her mother died, and now she was left in the care of her two half brothers who treated her like the dirt beneath their feet. Poor Jedida was the victim of a family conflict, and she could do nothing to change what happened.

Her brothers were filled with bitterness when their father took a second wife and showered her with affection. Shortly after the marriage, Jedida—whose name means "darling of Jehovah"—was born to the union. In spite of the ongoing conflict between the two wives, as a little girl Jedida lived a happy life. But after her father's first wife died of heartbreak and bitterness, the wrath of her two brothers reached new heights. They constantly argued with their father and refused to obey his orders. The perpetual struggle proved to be too much for her father to bear, and one day he fell over dead.

Of course, her mother was no match for these two young lions, but she stood her ground until her strength failed and she joined her husband in death. The revenge against Jedida was swift. They threw her out of the house without any money or a place to live. Fortunately, the elders of her village came to her rescue and forced her brothers to allow their half sister to remain at home. But not even the elders could stop them from hiring her out as a laborer in a nearby vineyard.

"You're ugly and worthless!" one brother snarled at her.

"No one will ever want you, and don't expect us to take care of you!" the second brother added.

As Jedida lay by the stream gathering strength to return to her labors, she looked with tear-filled eyes at her grimy hands and tattered dress. She was in a terrible dilemma with no hope that things would ever change. She was forced to submit to her brothers' cruelty or become a prostitute or beggar on the street. There was no chance for a young woman of her age to find decent work. She had no money for a dowry, so marriage was out of the question. In the mirror of her mind, she was exactly what her brothers called her—ugly, poor, and undesirable. She smelled of sweat and dirt and her ebony skin was baked and cracked like the earth when drought dries it to the core. Jedida lay weeping on the ground, wishing it were her grave.

Suddenly, the stillness of the earth was replaced with a distant rumbling. The thunderous sound was like a storm stirring on the horizon, but when Jedida looked up the sky was crystal clear. *What does this noise mean?* she thought. Moments later the answer to her question came into full view. A legion of soldiers galloped over the hillside, followed by a splendid chariot drawn by a team of white stallions. Jedida's heart pounded as the soldiers headed straight toward the stream to water their horses.

She tried not to panic as she slipped behind a tree and crouched down like a frightened child. But to her dismay a soldier with a face like a hungry bear discovered her hiding place. Jedida scrambled up the hill, running as fast as she could. But the soldier was much faster. He caught her by the ankle. She kicked her way free, then screamed as another soldier caught her by the back of her dress and locked her in his grip.

"Let her go!" a thunderous voice rang out.

The soldier quickly released his grip, but Jedida was too exhausted to run. She stood frozen in her tracks as the white horses and the golden chariot slowly rumbled down the hillside and stopped just inches from where she was standing. A man with copper skin and braided hair stared at her from his chariot.

Jedida fell to her knees and began to weep. "Please, have mercy on me. I am not a wicked woman. I was only getting water from the stream… I did nothing wrong."

The answer from the man in the chariot came as a complete surprise. "What is your name, fair lady?"

Her eyes were filled with wonder as she looked up at the regal stranger who was wearing an embroidered robe. "Jedida, sir."

"The Lord has blessed you this day," he said. "For surely God has sent me to rescue you from this parched vineyard."

Jedida thought she might be dreaming, but she was wide awake.

"Where is your family?" the man asked.

"I have no family," Jedida answered.

"Then who takes care of you?"

Jedida paused for a moment. "I have two half brothers, but…"
Tears fell.

"Say no more." The man with the look of royalty smiled from his carriage. "I want you to come with me to Jerusalem where you will be properly cared for. I will speak to your brothers when the time comes."

Without another word the man arrayed in a royal robe, gold earrings, and bracelets stretched out his hand to help Jedida into his chariot. "I am Solomon, king of Israel. You will be safe with me."

Jedida drew back with fear in her eyes. "But I can't! I'm too dirty. I'm nothing more than a peasant!" Her voice trembled.

Solomon smiled as he stepped out of his chariot and came close to the woman. Even the sweat and dirt that covered her skin could not hide her breathtaking beauty.

"Fair lady, I can clearly see that you are a queen who is only disguised as a peasant," he said softly. "There is not one blemish in you—for you are altogether lovely. Your eyes are as gentle as a dove."

Jedida bowed her head and wept as Solomon placed his beautiful robe over her shoulders. "I am not worthy of your kindness," she sobbed.

Solomon lifted her chin and looked into her dark eyes. "You are precious in my sight. You will wear a string of pearls around your neck and a crown upon your head, and everyone who looks at you will see your beauty."

Jedida smiled at the king. She was trembling with joy as she rode toward her new life in Jerusalem.

"Who is this maiden coming up from the wilderness, leaning upon her beloved?" one of Jedida's brothers asked when they saw the couple riding toward Jerusalem in the royal chariot. Of course neither of them recognized their beautiful sister, for she was covered with the royal cloak of her beloved.

This story, inspired by the Song of Solomon, reveals that the spirit of kindness is powerful. Lady Pearl knows that as she walks in the wisdom of God and applies his Word to her life (no matter how strange it might seem), she will always prevail.

Ms. Pearl is like an angel whose luminous smile tells you she is richly endowed with kindness. Pearl lets you go ahead of her in a crowded supermarket line. She comforts a child who is lost in the mall. She is patient with people who are rude and will sacrifice her own comfort for the sake of others. She is supportive of her husband, always walking by his side with kindness, encouragement, and wise counsel.

This godly woman with the qualities of a pearl is often misunderstood. Her kindness can be mistaken for weakness, but her wisdom and power speak clearly to those who lack spiritual understanding. With great kindness she will step out of the way of fools who are bent on self-destruction.

Two defining characteristics of a pearl are the smoothness of its surface and its luminous glow. Lady Pearl develops smoothness in her style. She is never rough or abrasive, nor is she ruffled by overwhelming circumstances. Her confidence in the Lord gives her a luminous glow because she spends time in the presence of the Lord. Each time she faces a difficulty, her face grows more beautiful with the wisdom of God.

Godly wisdom is a gift the Lord longs to give to each of us, but it comes through encounters with the best and worst of real-life experiences.

If you are a younger woman, make sure you have a relationship with an older woman who is filled with the spirit of wisdom. If you are an older woman, get connected to younger women so you can stay in touch with life in the here and now.

Proverbs 9 portrays wisdom as a beautiful woman who lives in a magnificent house and leaves her doors wide open to help those in need. Picture wisdom as a lovely Black woman, her arms outstretched to receive you into her house. "Wisdom has built her house; she has hewn out its seven pillars.... She calls from the highest point of the city. 'Let all who are simple come in here!' she says to those who lack judgment." (Proverbs 9:1-4, NIV).

Scripture tells us that Wisdom builds her house on seven pillars. Seven is the number of completion or fullness, and in ancient times a house that needed seven pillars was palatial.

A stone pillar cannot be moved by wind, rain, or hungry termites. Godly principles are no different. No matter how much time passes or how much a society changes, the principles remain the same. The following seven principles from Lady Wisdom serve to encourage us to strengthen our relationship with her:

1. Wisdom offers long life.

Happy is the [person] who finds wisdom,
And the [person] who gains understanding....
Length of days is in her right hand. (Proverbs 3:13,16a)

2. Wisdom offers riches and honor.

Happy is the [person] who finds wisdom....
In her left hand [are] riches and honor. (Proverbs 3:13,16b)

3. Wisdom offers power and leadership.

Wisdom strengthens the wise
More than ten rulers of the city. (Ecclesiastes 7:19)

4. Wisdom offers wise counsel.

I, wisdom, dwell with prudence,
And find out knowledge and discretion....
Counsel is mine,
And sound wisdom. (Proverbs 8:12,14)

5. Wisdom offers creativity.

The LORD by wisdom founded the earth;
By understanding He established the heavens. (Proverbs 3:19)

6. Wisdom offers knowledge.

The fear of the LORD is the beginning of wisdom,
And the knowledge of the Holy One is understanding. (Proverbs 9:10)

7. Wisdom offers protection.

Do not forsake [wisdom], and she will preserve you. (Proverbs 4:6)

Imitation pearls can be found at jewelry counters around the world. They have no real value and almost anyone can afford to buy them. They are mere glass covered with a pretty layer of pearlescence. With time and wear the covering will peel away, exposing the dull glass beneath the surface. A woman who speaks wise words but gets involved in foolish deeds is like a string of counterfeit pearls. So is a woman who talks about kindness but is never available when help is needed. The Bible says you will know them by their fruits (see Matthew 7:16).

The Bible also tells us there are two types of wisdom, earthly and heavenly:

> But if you harbor bitter envy and selfish ambition in your hearts, do not boast about it or deny the truth. Such "wisdom" does not come down from heaven but is earthly, unspiritual, of the devil. (James 3:14-15, NIV)

> But the wisdom that comes from heaven is first of all pure; then peace-loving, considerate, submissive, full of mercy and good fruit, impartial and sincere. (James 3:17, NIV)

Some people employ ungodly wisdom to achieve an evil purpose. For example, con artists, corrupt politicians, and lawyers use ungodly wisdom to their advantage. In the first chapter of Romans, the apostle Paul calls such people "inventors of evil things" (verse 30).

The evidence of godly wisdom is purity, peace, and kindness. But if you operate in godly wisdom, be careful not to allow pride and arrogance to change your heart. In the days of his youth, King Solomon was filled with godly wisdom. His wisdom led him to become wealthy and famous. But pride in all of his accomplishments and the absence of wise counsel caused him to become arrogant and rebellious toward God.

Heed the warnings of Solomon's sin and pray that the blessings from the Lord will never corrupt the beautiful spirit of wisdom that dwells within your heart. Also surround yourself with wise counselors.

I am convinced that God allows irritating and uncomfortable intrusion to enter the shell of our lives so that we will continue to produce pearly layers of wisdom and kindness and to be humble and dependant upon his mercy and grace. The wise woman who produces beautiful pearls in her life will not only cherish what the Lord has given her but pass on her pearls of wisdom to those who share her life.

Here are some valued pearls of wisdom that have been passed on to me by the women I hold dear:

Shelley Jones, my great-grandmother: "It's a lot easier to give people advice when you feed them and tell them a story first."

Barbara Prunty, my mother: "Every child is entitled to a childhood. Make sure you give your children a happy childhood so they can be happy adults."

Dr. Juanita Smith, pastor: "When God says 'nevertheless,' it means that he will never give you the less but more."

Bunny Wilson, author and speaker: "There's no way to judge your commitment to God until you live your life God's way."

Michelle McKinney Hammond, author: "Perhaps when we don't feel God beside us, he's simply leaving room for us to grow."

Janet Bailey, codirector of Women's Discipleship Group: "Sometimes you have to step back and let people learn about life the hard way."

Pat Ashley, speaker: "Endurance is the ability not just to bear a hard thing but to turn it into victory and glory."

Nichole stood on the subway platform fully engrossed in her book on assertiveness training. She was tired of living a life where her kindness was taken for weakness. She was always being pushed around and overlooked for the best jobs and even the best guys. Nichole didn't understand why she was the one who took the smaller bedroom in the apartment she shared with two roommates yet had to pay an extra twenty-five dollars each month. She was demoted at her job because she shared her idea with a coworker who then got the credit for it. Finally, Nichole had no money in the bank because she gave her savings to her gorgeous younger sister so she could realize her dream of taking acting lessons.

For a long time she didn't know if she was just plain stupid or perhaps she simply needed to wise up and figure out how to change her life for the better. Now as she stood on the subway platform waiting for the train that would take her downtown to her job in the mailroom, she was ready to take the first step to becoming more assertive.

The book she was reading gave the following advice: "Life is one big competition. If you learn to win at the smaller games, then you'll be ready to play for higher stakes. Example: If the line is too long at the market checkout stand, demand that they open a second line."

Nichole couldn't believe her eyes as she read the next piece of advice: "If you're riding public transportation, be the one who gets the only vacant seat. Make it your quest!"

Nichole's heart leaped with excitement as she looked down the subway track and saw the distant headlights from the approaching train.

Be the one who gets the only vacant seat! Make it your quest! Nichole repeated the words over and over to herself as the train roared down the track. "I'm tired of being a loser. Today is my day, and I'm going to get my seat!" she screamed inside of herself.

As the train slowed to a stop and the doors opened, for a moment Nichole froze as she thought about her quest. A man in a business suit pushed her out of the way as he made his exit. "Hey! Watch it!" Nichole whined as another faceless body spun her around. The stampede of commuters pushed her onboard. The doors closed and the train jerked forward. Nichole pulled herself together and tried to focus as she moved down the aisle. Her heart was beating fast as she looked around for the seat that belonged to her and her alone. Not too far away she spotted an unoccupied square of blue vinyl. But how would she maneuver her way down an aisle filled with a hostile army of commuters?

Once again the words from her book on assertiveness training flashed in her mind. *Be the one who gets the vacant seat. Make it your quest!*

"Excuse me—I beg your pardon—can I slip by you, please?" These words quickly gave way to: "Coming through—watch your feet—suck it in, folks—move it or lose it!" Nichole felt as though she were having an out-of-body experience as the empty seat came into full view. Suddenly the train hit a sharp turn, and she went flying onto the lap of a young man with green hair and a nose ring. "Are you married?" she laughed as he grabbed her before she hit the floor.

Nichole was delirious with power. *So this is how the other half lives,* she thought. She regained her balance and ran to claim the empty vinyl seat.

"Hey, I was here first!" A construction worker challenged the victor.

"You wish!" Nichole glared at him. The man grumbled and then backed off.

As she settled into the narrow seat, a vision flashed into her head. She was standing on the Olympic podium with a bouquet of flowers in her arms. She was almost in tears as they called her name and presented her with a gold medal. The crowd roared with delight—actually it was the sound of the subway rumbling down the track.

Nichole smiled as she opened her book and began to read. She glanced up and saw an elderly woman struggling to hold onto the pole. From where Nicole was sitting she could see that the woman's ankles were badly swollen. She tried not to listen to the wimpy voice inside pleading with Nichole to give this poor woman her seat. Finally, she gave in.

"Would you like to sit down?" Nichole asked the frail-looking woman.

"Thank you, dear. How nice of you to give me your seat."

Nichole stood up with pride. Holding the pole tightly, she swayed back and forth like a palm tree as once again she opened her book on assertiveness training. She smiled as she read the words: "While you should never allow yourself to be manipulated by people, always apply the law of kindness whenever possible."

Therefore, as God's chosen people,
holy and dearly loved, clothe yourselves
with compassion, kindness, humility,
gentleness and patience.

COLOSSIANS 3:12, NIV

Chapter 17

The Gift of Precious Jewels

Treasures That Never Fade

Each one should use whatever gift he has received to serve others,
faithfully administering God's grace in its various forms.

1 PETER 4:10, NIV

The first jewel I ever received was an heirloom my mother bestowed on me when I was thirteen years old. It is an engagement ring, a small diamond set in sterling silver that once belonged to my grandmother. The ring was passed to my mother, and when she married it was passed to her younger sister. The tradition continued until the ring reached my anxious fingers. I felt I had finally reached womanhood. But with the ring came an unspoken responsibility to uphold the reputation and dignity of the women in our family. That small diamond ring meant I was loved, accepted, and treasured by my family.

The second jewel I was given came from my husband. It was a diamond wedding ring, a yellow gold band with a large round diamond in the center and three smaller diamonds on each side. Wearing that ring felt like waving a flag to announce that I was loved by a handsome, milk chocolate, financially secure, loving-me-all-the-time Black man. Whenever someone asked about my beautiful ring, I seized the chance to tell that person about Adam, the man who loved me enough to give me the very best.

The third jewel given to me came from one of my dearest friends, Juanita. It was a beautiful cross of red rubies set in gold. Juanita and I had been best friends for almost twenty years when she gave me that lovely cross for a birthday present. For me it was a reminder of the importance and value of our friendship. We had our fun and fights, yet our friendship endured like the precious red rubies that hung around my neck.

The first two jewels I gave were to my precious daughters, Roslyn and Theresa, each on their thirteenth birthdays. Theresa loved her diamond earrings and matching diamond necklace. Roslyn's eyes lit up when I gave her a ring with an opal set in gold. At first I was afraid they would lose their jewelry, and I always reminded them to take good care of it. But as time passed, I learned an important lesson. When people appreciate a gift, they take good care of it. Over the years, neither of my daughters has misplaced or lost the jewels I gave them, nor have they lost the love that came with the gifts.

The gift of a jewel is more than a trinket to add to your adornment and status. It is a symbol of the love and value that we place on our relationships with one another. Even if you have never received the gift of a gemstone, you can lay claim to other types of jewels that time can never destroy. For example, I consider my daughters the most precious jewels I have ever possessed. I wouldn't trade them for all the rubies and diamonds in the world.

I can also think of moments in my life that are like precious jewels forever hidden in my heart. The first time my husband and I were apart for a whole week was an unforgettable experience. When I flew home on New Year's Eve, he was waiting for me at the airport with a bouquet of red roses in hand. We hugged and kissed for what seemed an eternity. Then we went to church that night and prayed in the new year. Afterward we went home and danced to music on the radio. That night is a jewel I will treasure forever.

On another occasion, I traveled with my mother and father, my two daughters, and my nephew to our hometown of Philadelphia for a family gathering. There's nothing better than a noisy Black family reunion. My children had a chance to meet their great aunts, uncles, and cousins. We took a good look at their body structures, facial features, hair and skin color, and clearly saw our own reflections. We had the best time laughing with the old and the young, taking family pictures, dancing the electric slide, and eating fried chicken, greens, and potato salad. We ended the day holding hands and praying for one another. This jewel will shine in my memory forever.

Sitting across the dinner table from Martin Luther King Jr. and listening to his jokes is a snapshot moment that I will treasure forever.

More recently, I walked across the graduation stage to receive my master's degree in theology with my family looking on. What a shining moment!

You, too, have a treasure trove of precious jewels, if only you have eyes to see them. Perhaps someone shared words you will never forget. When I was fourteen and going through a difficult time, Mother Myles, a minister in our church, saw me crying at the altar one Sunday morning. She whispered in my ear, "Don't let anybody steal your joy."

Her words didn't seem profound at the time, but they never left me. To this day, I guard myself against situations that steal my joy. Those words were set in the breastplate of my heart forever.

Think about your life and your jewels. Find twelve precious people or moments in your life to place as jewels in your own personal breastplate.

It might be a teacher, a parent, or even a passing stranger who came to your rescue. Personal jewels come disguised in many ways. Sometimes you have to dig through the rocks of disappointment and hurt to see the value of what you really have.

As you dig for your spiritual jewels—the Lord's richest blessings in your life—here's a list of precious gems that will make you wealthy indeed. (There may be jewels that I have overlooked. Please add yours to the list.)

- **Salvation:** Knowing the Lord is the richest blessing you could ever have.
- **Love:** Having someone to love and loving in return is a gift from God.
- **Family:** They are a gift from God we often take for granted or overlook.
- **Friends:** Life is wonderful because of the laughter and support of friends.
- **Children:** Whether they belong to you or not, all children make life beautiful.
- **Elders:** Their wisdom about life gives us the love and guidance we need.
- **Work:** The chance to prosper and express our creative ideas is a blessing.
- **Celebrations:** Weddings, birthdays, Christmas, and anniversaries make life fun.
- **Health:** This is a blessing that only God can give. So are those who help the sick.
- **Service:** Helping others will bless you as well as those in need of help.

- **Peace:** A free and safe nation and a heart that is at rest is a blessing.
- **Wealth:** Having enough to meet your needs and to help others is a blessing.

Dig deep in your memory to discover every hidden gift, then record your treasures in a decorative book and put it in a safe place. Treat your book with the same care you would give diamonds and pearls. Show off your jewels by sharing those wonderful people and experiences with others. Be sure to thank the people who made sacrifices for you and blessed you with precious memories.

Then pray and thank the Lord for making you so wealthy. Pray for the people in your book of jewels. If you have more than twelve jewels to write about, praise the Lord! You are wealthy indeed.

Keep your jewel book handy in case tomorrow you strike it rich in terms of your personal experiences. A sudden turn of events might be like a shower of emeralds, pearls, diamonds, and sapphires falling into your lap. The Lord loves to surprise us, especially when we're hanging on by a thread.

As you reflect on the blessings God has bestowed, take time not only to count the precious jewels you've gathered, but also to reflect on the ways you can share your treasures and bring beauty to the life of another.

The greatest gift we bring to one another across racial lines is our diversity. I am blessed to know women of different racial and ethnic backgrounds who are like precious jewels. Spanish, Asian, Arab, Jewish, Irish. I count them all among my most precious friends. Rosie Sicra, a beautiful

Spanish lady, shines like a diamond. Tess Cox, my close Irish friend, is as refreshing as a bright green emerald. Helen Lim is a fun-filled Korean sister whose gentle spirit and passion for worshiping God is like a flaming ruby. These sisters in the faith are involved in ministry to women and have been a tremendous blessing to my life. They are just a few of the jewels that God has allowed me to place in my personal treasure chest.

Another friend I treasure is Philine, a beautiful Chinese lady from Singapore who often shares with me the stories she writes about children. I encountered another precious gem when my daughter became very ill and was referred to Dr. Parisa Marada, a wonderful Iranian lady. Not only is she a brilliant doctor, but she also became a warm and caring friend. Parisa is Muslim, yet I prayed with her concerning a pressing issue in her life. If ever there was a jewel given to my daughter and me by the Lord, it was Dr. Marada.

One of the most important gifts we can give women of other ethnic backgrounds is our tribal heritage. We are not a racial group that blends in to the beige complexions of the world. Our rainbow of complexions definitely stands out. Know who you are in Christ and be joyful that as Black women of God we are "fearfully and wonderfully made" (Psalm 139:14).

When people are curious about you, your looks, culture, cooking, and family lifestyle, become an ambassador—a jewel on the breastplate of your High Priest, Jesus Christ. Do not feel intruded upon when other women ask about the texture of your hair or why you have problems with your extra "trunk space" when it comes to wearing certain brands of designer jeans. Use their interest as opportunities to show the beauty and uniqueness of God's creation.

When you are confident about the woman the Lord created you to be, there is no reason to be offended. Give others the gift of knowing a beautiful Black sister who is loving, kind, and respectful of all people. Have a godly and global view. You might even meet the man of your dreams if you dare to venture across racial lines!

Don't allow the demons of prejudice to cause you to miss a wonderful gift from the Lord. Discrimination creates division among our own ranks as women of African ancestry. Caribbean women find themselves at odds with African-American women. Native African women can be distrustful of their Euro-African sisters. Rich ignore poor, even within families. Complexion and hair texture cause envy and strife between sisters. Deeply ingrained prejudices can damage the self-esteem of young Black girls. When one girl is shown preference based on skin color or hair texture, another is made to feel rejected and inferior.

But sizes, shapes, colors, and age are nothing more than the beautiful velvet box that holds a precious jewel. Why waste time making a judgment about the "box" when it's the jewel inside that matters?

We must do all in our power to stamp out the practice of brutal name-calling even in joking. Family members who allow—or worse, participate in—this kind of abuse inflict damage that scars for life. Many times family environment, not outside racism, robs young Black women of their God-given gifts and talents. Be sure to give the gift of encouraging words to a young person who needs to know she is special and beautiful.

Encouragement and affirmation from a supportive family allow young Black women to shine brightly as precious jewels. When you are made to feel beautiful and loved, it doesn't matter if your hair is short and woolly, your nose wide, and your lips full. You have the confidence to become a top fashion model, because the beauty inside of you was encouraged to flourish.

How many times have you looked at your own reflection in the mirror and said something negative? You wouldn't tell a friend she looks terrible. Don't say negative things to the person who matters the most—you! Consider yourself carefully. The next time you look in the mirror, I want you to say something like this:

> Hey there, I am so glad to see my favorite person. Sometimes I get so busy that I forget how valuable and special you are. You are a gift from God—a rare treasure. Therefore, you must never mistreat yourself. Make sure you take care of your health and learn how to rest and relax. Never carelessly put yourself in the position to have your hopes and dreams stolen or lost. Every part of your being, inside and out, is a custom design. Each day your fabulous mind opens you up to new adventures and new challenges. Your spirit is linked to your heavenly Father, and he reveals his plan and purpose for your life. You are the beloved daughter of the One who created the universe. You are of royal birth—heir to a vast inheritance. You are a jewel, precious and valuable in every way. If others look at you and don't see how beautiful you really are, it's because they have not yet acquired the knowledge and discernment to recognize a priceless gift when they see one.

When you search your heart, you will find that you are endowed with some of the attributes of every jewel that God has created. In the book of Ephesians, the apostle Paul prays this for every believer: "that you may be filled with all the fullness of God" (3:19).

When we have been "filled with all the fullness of God," we lack nothing. We have the strength of a diamond, the faith of a sapphire, the grace of a turquoise, and the wisdom of a pearl. As we pass through the phases of life, we balance the dreams of opal with the soberness of amethyst. We will develop the good judgment of emerald, but never lose the happiness of onyx or the vision of topaz. As godly women, we walk in the virtue of ruby and experience the peace of aquamarine. Finally, agate grants us forgetfulness concerning the past and complete faith that what the future holds for each of us is nothing less than incredible, miraculous, and divine.

Every good gift and every perfect gift is from above,
and comes down from the Father of lights,
with whom there is no variation or shadow of turning.

JAMES 1:17

Suggested Reading List

Brown–Driver–Briggs. *Hebrew and English Lexicon.* Peabody, Mass.: Henderson, 1996.

Butler, John C. "Gem by Gem." www.worldbookonline.com.

Desautels, Paul E. *The Gem Kingdom.* New York: Random House, 1970.

Driver, S. R. *Notes on the Hebrew Text of the Books of Samuel,* Oxford: Clarendon, 1913.

Easton, M. H. *12 Tribes. Illustrated Bible Dictionary.* Nashville: Thomas Nelson, 1986.

Ely, Patrick Melvin. *The Adventures of Amos 'n' Andy.* Charlottesville: University Press of Virginia, 2002.

Fage, J. D. *A History of Africa.* New York: Rutledge, 1997.

Fisher, P. J. *The Science of Gems.* New York: Charles Scribner's Sons, 1966.

Gait, Ph.D., R. I. "Rubies and Sapphires." *A General Guide.* Toronto: Department of Mineralogy, Royal Ontario Museum, 1969.

de Geus, C. H. J. *The Tribes of Israel.* Assen: Van Gorcum, 1976.

Gross, Felix. *Rhodes of Africa.* New York: Frederick A. Praeger, 1957.

Hart, Matthew. *Diamond: A Journey to the Heart.* New York: Walker, 2001.

Hoffman, Richard J. "Pearls." www.worldbookonline.com.

Jackson, Guida M. *Women Who Ruled.* Santa Barbara, Calif.: ABC-CLIO, 1998.

Jones, David E. *Women Warriors: a History.* Washington: Brassey's, 1997.

Kohlenberger III, John R., ed. *Hebrew-English Old Testament.* Grand Rapids, Mich.: Zondervan, 1979–1985.

Kraus, Ransy D. "World Jewelry." www.worldbookonline.com.

Lewis, Jone Johnson. *Biographies—Famous Black Women in History.* www.thehistorynet.com.

Millar, William R. *The Priesthood of Ancient Israel.* St. Louis: Chalice, 2001.

Patton, Venetria K. *Women in Chains (Legacy of Slavery).* Albany: New York University Press, 2000.

Pederson, Jay P., and Estell, Kenneth, eds. "The 700 Best Known Africans." *African American Almanac,* Detroit: UXL, 1994.

Pritchard, James B. "Solomon and Sheba." *Ancient Near Eastern Texts: Relating to the Old Testament.* Princeton: Princeton University Press, 1958.

Rapaport, Martin. "Diamonds in Conflict." Global Policy Forum. January 2003.

Rowley, H. H. *The Faith of Israel.* Philadelphia: Westminster Press, 1957.

Tully, Thomas. *Sons of Jacob.* New York: Doran, 19–.

For a Study Guide
with questions suitable
for individual or group use,
please visit www.terrimcfaddin.org.

About the Author

TERRI MCFADDIN became a Christian in 1975 and is a Bible teacher and ordained minister. She holds a master's degree in theology from Fuller Theological Seminary and is the author of *God Made Me Beauty-full* and *Only a Woman*. A speaker, playwright, and songwriter with two Grammy Awards to her credit, Terri spent ten years as a Motown songwriter and has penned songs for many popular Christian artists.

In 1999, Terri organized Women's Discipleship Group, a teaching ministry that prepares women for service in various areas of ministry. She has also served as chaplain for the Christian Entertainers of Southern California, as well as on the board of the Los Angeles County Commission on Women.

Terri resides in Altadena, California, and is a member of Faithful Central Bible Church. She is a widow and the proud mother of two adult daughters, Roslyn McFaddin Ballard and Theresa McFaddin, who is also an ordained minister.

To contact Terri McFaddin or to learn more about her ministries, please visit www.terrimcfaddin.org.

To learn more about WaterBrook Press and view
our catalog of products, log on to our Web site:
www.waterbrookpress.com

WATERBROOK
PRESS